W9-BUA-388

"This series is a tremendous resource for those wanting to study and teach the Bible with an understanding of how the gospel is woven throughout Scripture. Here are gospel-minded pastors and scholars doing gospel business from all the Scriptures. This is a biblical and theological feast preparing God's people to apply the entire Bible to all of life with heart and mind wholly committed to Christ's priorities."

> **BRYAN CHAPELL,** President Emeritus, Covenant Theological Seminary; Senior Pastor, Grace Presbyterian Church, Peoria, Illinois

"Mark Twain may have smiled when he wrote to a friend, 'I didn't have time to write you a short letter, so I wrote you a long letter.' But the truth of Twain's remark remains serious and universal, because well-reasoned, compact writing requires extra time and extra hard work. And this is what we have in the Crossway Bible study series *Knowing the Bible*. The skilled authors and notable editors provide the contours of each book of the Bible as well as the grand theological themes that bind them together as one Book. Here, in a 12-week format, are carefully wrought studies that will ignite the mind and the heart."

> **R. KENT HUGHES,** Visiting Professor of Practical Theology, Westminster Theological Seminary

"*Knowing the Bible* brings together a gifted team of Bible teachers to produce a high-quality series of study guides. The coordinated focus of these materials is unique: biblical content, provocative questions, systematic theology, practical application, and the gospel story of God's grace presented all the way through Scripture."

> **PHILIP G. RYKEN,** President, Wheaton College

"These *Knowing the Bible* volumes provide a significant and very welcome variation on the general run of inductive Bible studies. This series provides substantial instruction, as well as teaching through the very questions that are asked. *Knowing the Bible* then goes even further by showing how any given text links with the gospel, the whole Bible, and the formation of theology. I heartily endorse this orientation of individual books to the whole Bible and the gospel, and I applaud the demonstration that sound theology was not something invented later by Christians, but is right there in the pages of Scripture."

> **GRAEME L. GOLDSWORTHY,** former lecturer, Moore Theological College; author, *According to Plan*, *Gospel and Kingdom*, *The Gospel in Revelation*, and *Gospel and Wisdom*

"What a gift to earnest, Bible-loving, Bible-searching believers! The organization and structure of the Bible study format presented through the *Knowing the Bible* series is so well conceived. Students of the Word are led to understand the content of passages through perceptive, guided questions, and they are given rich insights and application all along the way in the brief but illuminating sections that conclude each study. What potential growth in depth and breadth of understanding these studies offer! One can only pray that vast numbers of believers will discover more of God and the beauty of his Word through these rich studies."

> **BRUCE A. WARE,** Professor of Christian Theology, The Southern Baptist Theological Seminary

KNOWING THE BIBLE

J. I. Packer, Theological Editor
Dane C. Ortlund, Series Editor
Lane T. Dennis, Executive Editor

•   •   •   •   •   •

Genesis	Ecclesiastes	John	Colossians,
Exodus	Isaiah	Acts	Philemon
Leviticus	Jeremiah	Romans	Hebrews
Joshua	Daniel	1 Corinthians	James
Ruth, Esther	Hosea	2 Corinthians	Revelation
Ezra, Nehemiah	Matthew	Galatians	
Psalms	Mark	Ephesians	
Proverbs	Luke	Philippians	

•   •   •   •   •   •

J. I. PACKER is Board of Governors' Professor of Theology at Regent College (Vancouver, BC). Dr. Packer earned his DPhil at the University of Oxford. He is known and loved worldwide as the author of the best-selling book *Knowing God*, as well as many other titles on theology and the Christian life. He serves as the General Editor of the ESV Bible and as the Theological Editor for the *ESV Study Bible*.

LANE T. DENNIS is President of Crossway, a not-for-profit publishing ministry. Dr. Dennis earned his PhD from Northwestern University. He is Chair of the ESV Bible Translation Oversight Committee and Executive Editor of the *ESV Study Bible*.

DANE C. ORTLUND is Executive Vice President of Bible Publishing and Bible Publisher at Crossway. He is a graduate of Covenant Theological Seminary (MDiv, ThM) and Wheaton College (BA, PhD). Dr. Ortlund has authored several books and scholarly articles in the areas of Bible, theology, and Christian living.

JOHN

A 12-WEEK STUDY

Justin Buzzard

:: CROSSWAY®

WHEATON, ILLINOIS

TABLE OF CONTENTS

▲

SERIES PREFACE

KNOWING THE BIBLE, as the series title indicates, was created to help readers know and understand the meaning, the message, and the God of the Bible. Each volume in the series consists of 12 units that progressively take the reader through a clear, concise study of that book of the Bible. In this way, any given volume can fruitfully be used in a 12-week format either in group study, such as in a church-based context, or in individual study. Of course, these 12 studies could be completed in fewer or more than 12 weeks, as convenient, depending on the context in which they are used.

Each study unit gives an overview of the text at hand before digging into it with a series of questions for reflection or discussion. The unit then concludes by highlighting the gospel of grace in each passage ("Gospel Glimpses"), identifying whole-Bible themes that occur in the passage ("Whole-Bible Connections"), and pinpointing Christian doctrines that are affirmed in the passage ("Theological Soundings").

The final component to each unit is a section for reflecting on personal and practical implications from the passage at hand. The layout provides space for recording responses to the questions proposed, and we think readers need to do this to get the full benefit of the exercise. The series also includes definitions of key words. These definitions are indicated by a note number in the text and are found at the end of each chapter.

Lastly, to help understand the Bible in this deeper way, we urge readers to use the ESV Bible and the *ESV Study Bible*, which are available in various print and digital formats, including online editions at www.esvbible.org. The *Knowing the Bible* series is also available online. Additional 12-week studies covering each book of the Bible will be added as they become available.

May the Lord greatly bless your study as you seek to know him through knowing his Word.

J. I. Packer

Lane T. Dennis

Week 1: Overview

▲

Getting Acquainted

The Gospel of John plays a unique and influential role in the Christian Bible. In this account of the life, death, and resurrection of Jesus, we learn that Jesus is the Son of God,[1] sent[2] by God the Father to give eternal life[3] to all who believe in him. Jesus repeatedly shatters people's assumptions, teaching that salvation is not earned but rather is a free gift received through a miracle of grace—being born again. John's Gospel also sounds a constant theme of mission. Just as the Father sent Jesus to earth, Jesus sends his followers to continue his mission by testifying that Jesus is the Son of God so that "whoever believes in him should not perish but have eternal life" (3:16).

Of the four Gospels, John was probably the last one written. It is the most theologically and philosophically profound Gospel account. John does not narrate Jesus' birth. Instead, he begins his Gospel at the very beginning, stating in his opening sentence that Jesus has eternally existed and that "all things were made through him" (1:3). John roots Jesus' identity in eternity past, providing a lofty vision of the Son of God sent to earth as fully God and now also fully man. Other than the feeding of the five thousand, the anointing at Bethany (12:1–8), and the passion narrative, John does not share any sizable blocks of teaching with the Synoptic Gospels. John is organized around carefully crafted narrative strands that highlight both the signs and teachings of Jesus. This gives John's Gospel a sense of depth as the reader is presented with a rich, multi-layered, and cosmic display of the identity, works, words, and mission of Jesus.

John's purpose is to present Jesus as the Messiah, the Son of God, sent to earth to fulfill all that the Old Testament anticipated: bringing new life—eternal life—to a dark world.

Placing It in the Larger Story

While Matthew focuses on Jesus as the Jewish Messiah, Mark focuses on Jesus as the one who ushers in the kingdom of God, and Luke emphasizes Jesus as the one who welcomes the outsider, John emphasizes Jesus as the eternal Son of God. Through his signs and teaching, through his death and resurrection, and through the mission he entrusts to his disciples, Jesus fulfills all the Old Testament hopes and promises. He inaugurates the long-awaited new age.

Key Passage

"Now Jesus did many other signs in the presence of the disciples, which are not written in this book; but these are written so that you may believe that Jesus is the Christ, the Son of God, and that by believing you may have life in his name" (John 20:30–31).

Date and Historical Background

The Gospel of John was written by the apostle John, the son of Zebedee. He was a Palestinian Jew and a member of Jesus' inner apostolic circle. John most likely wrote his account of Jesus between AD 70 (when Jerusalem was besieged by the Romans and the temple was destroyed) and AD 100 (the approximate end of John's lifetime). Most likely he wrote his Gospel in Ephesus, one of the most important urban centers of the Roman empire. John's Gospel was aimed at both Jews and Gentiles living throughout the Greco-Roman world. John frequently explains Jewish customs and Palestinian geography to non-Jewish readers. John also presents Jesus as the eternal Word that has now become flesh, utilizing the background of Greek thought familiar to his Gentile audience. Yet John clearly also has a Jewish audience in mind: he reveals Jesus to be the Jewish Messiah, the fulfillment of many Old Testament themes, and the eternal Son of God sent by God the Father to mediate a new relationship between God and man.

John thus wrote his Gospel about two generations after the death and resurrection of Jesus. At the time of writing, the other three Gospels had been written and the Greco-Roman world was in a state of change. Jerusalem had been sacked by Rome. Jews were increasingly dispersed throughout the Roman empire, causing Jews and Gentiles to come into even more frequent contact. It is to this mixed and dispersed Jewish and Gentile audience that John directed his Gospel.

Outline

  I. Prologue: The Incarnate Word (1:1–18)

 II. The Signs of the Messiah (1:19–12:50)

    A. John the Baptist and the start of Jesus' ministry (1:19–2:11)

    B. Jesus' expanding ministry (2:12–4:54)

    C. More signs amid mounting Jewish opposition (5:1–10:42)

    D. The final Passover: the ultimate sign (11:1–12:19)

    E. The Messiah's death at hand (12:20–50)

III. The Farewell Discourse and the Passion Narrative (13:1–20:31)

    A. Jesus' final teaching and prayer (13:1–17:26)

    B. Jesus' arrest, trials, death, and burial (18:1–19:42)

    C. Jesus' resurrection and appearances (20:1–29)

    D. Purpose statement and epilogue (20:30–21:25)

As you get started . . .

What is your general understanding of the role of John's Gospel related to the other three Gospels? Do you have any sense of what John uniquely contributes?

John emphasizes Jesus as Eternal Son of God. Jesus' fulfillment. Inaugurates new age. Aimed at both Jews & Gentiles. Mixed audience. Both Jews & Greeks

How do you understand John's contribution to Christian theology? From your current knowledge of John, what does this account of the life of Jesus teach us about God, humanity, sin, redemption, and other doctrines?

John talks alot about love. Agape
Compassion

_I am_

What has perplexed you about John's Gospel? Are there any confusing parts to this Gospel that you would like to resolve as you begin this study of John?

They [?] will be with you always
the way [?] [?] God
Eternal life
John 17:26
Teaching on hell
"I am" teaching

> ## As You Finish This Unit . . .

Take a moment now to ask for the Lord's blessing and help as you engage in this study of John. And take a moment also to look back through this unit of study, to reflect on a few key things that you would like to learn throughout this study of John.

Definitions

[1] **Son of God** – Designates Jesus as the Messiah predicted in the Old Testament (2 Sam. 7:14; Ps. 2:7). This term gathers up many strands of Old Testament expectation about a coming "anointed one" who would lead and rescue God's people.

[2] **Sent** – John's favorite designation of Jesus is to call him the Son of God "sent" by the Father. This is set against a Jewish background in which a messenger represents the sender himself. Jesus is the ultimate "sent one"; he is the perfect revelation of God.

[3] **Eternal life** – For believers, the new life that begins with trust in Jesus Christ alone for salvation, and that continues after physical death for all eternity in God's presence in heaven.

WEEK 2:
PROLOGUE: THE
INCARNATE WORD

John 1:1–18

▲

This opening passage of John sets the stage for the rest of the Gospel. John opens with the words "In the beginning was the Word, and the Word was with God, and the Word was God" (1:1). From his very first sentence John proclaims that Jesus is the eternal, preexistent Word[1]—the one-of-a-kind Son of the Father, the Son who is himself God. Yet this eternal Word has now become incarnate[2] in history (1:11–18). In this prologue John introduces many of the major themes developed later in the Gospel, such as Jesus as the life, the light, and the truth; believers as God's children; and the world's rejection of Jesus. These first eighteen verses are the grand entryway into John's breathtaking account of Jesus Christ.

The Big Picture

John 1:1–18 shows us the good news that Jesus is God and that he has taken on flesh and come to earth as the fulfillment of all the promises of the Old Testament.

Reflection and Discussion

Read through the complete passage for this study, John 1:1–18. Then think through and write your own notes on the following questions. (For further background, see the *ESV Study Bible*, pages 2019–2020; also available online at www.esvbible.org.)

John roots the opening verses of his Gospel in the opening verses of Genesis. Compare John 1:1–5 with Genesis 1:1–5. What parallels do you see, and what do these parallels teach us about the message John wants his readers to hear?

Times -faith .

The Gospel of John has a different starting place than the other Gospels. Look briefly at the opening verses of Matthew, Mark, and Luke. What is unique about the opening of John's Gospel?

John 1:14 makes clear that when John speaks of "the Word," he is speaking of Jesus. Thus, John begins his Gospel by providing a lofty portrait of Jesus: revealing that Jesus is God, giving glimpses of the Trinitarian[3] nature of God, and teaching that Jesus was crucially involved in the very creation of the universe. List everything we learn about Jesus in these opening verses (1:1–5).

Continuing to draw upon Genesis motifs, John speaks about Jesus as the "life" and "light" who has come to shine in a dark world. What do John 8:12 and 10:10 teach us about the life and light we receive in Jesus?

In verse 6 we read that "there was a man sent from God, whose name was John" (this is John the Baptist—not to be confused with the author of this Gospel). According to verses 6–8 and 15, what was John's role and ambition?

According to verse 11, Jesus came "to his own, and his own people" (the Jews) "did not receive him." From what you know from the rest of Scripture, both Old Testament and New Testament, what are a few other instances where God's people reject God?

What do verses 9–13 teach about how to become a child of God? Where do you see God's grace[4] in these verses?

Verse 14 announces the greatest event in human history: the eternal, omnipotent Son of God took on human nature and lived among humanity as one who was both fully God and fully man at the same time, in one person. Before Jesus, who were some others who were sent from God to bring deliverance to God's people? In his mission to bring light and life to a dark and dying world, why is it critical that Jesus be both fully God and fully man?

Verse 14 speaks of the "glory" of Jesus. Read Exodus 33:18–23 and Deuteronomy 5:22–27. What do these passages teach us about what glory is, and about what John is communicating with his words, "we have seen his glory"?

Note verse 17. This verse is not drawing a contrast between law and grace in the sense that the Mosaic law was bad and Jesus is good. Rather, John is stating that both the giving of the law and the arrival of Jesus mark decisive events in the history of salvation. Through the law, God revealed his righteous character and requirements. Through Jesus, however, God reveals himself most fully, displaying his grace-soaked mission to meet the demands of the law for a dark world that has broken his law. What is superior about Jesus' ministry over Moses' ministry? What did Jesus accomplish that Moses did not—could not—accomplish?

Jesus fulfilled the laws.

Read through the following three sections on *Gospel Glimpses, Whole-Bible Connections,* and *Theological Soundings.* Then take time to reflect on the *Personal Implications* these sections may have for your walk with the Lord.

Gospel Glimpses

GOOD NEWS. These opening paragraphs of John's Gospel announce good news. Note that these first eighteen verses contain not a single command to obey, but simply news to believe. Consistent with the overarching story line of the Bible, this Gospel begins with gospel—with the good news that God has taken on flesh to rescue sinners living in a dark world. This is the resounding theme of John: good news. Jesus has come so that we, the undeserving, might receive "grace upon grace" (1:16).

PROMISES KEPT. John shows that Jesus is the fulfillment of Old Testament promises. We see the grace of God in his commitment to keep his promises to his people, despite their rebellion. "I will be your God, and you shall be my people" was a constant refrain throughout the Old Testament (e.g., Ex. 6:7; Lev. 26:12; Jer. 7:23). Yet God's people were consistently faithless, giving God every reason to cancel his promises. Nevertheless, "the Word became flesh and dwelt among us" (1:14). Despite our wickedness, God became flesh—he set up residence in a first-century Middle Eastern neighborhood—in order to be our God and save us. God keeps his promises.

CHILDREN OF GOD. These opening verses proclaim the best news in the world: estranged sinners can become God's children. How does one become a child of God? Not through turning in a resume or an application, or through some process of proving yourself worthy. John tells us we become God's children simply through believing in Jesus as God works in us the miracle of new birth: "But to all who did receive him, who believed in his name, he gave the right to become

15

children of God, who were born, not of blood nor of the will of the flesh nor of the will of man, but of God" (1:12–13). Anyone can become a child of God. All it takes is trusting in Christ.

Whole-Bible Connections

IN THE BEGINNING. John begins where the Bible begins. Genesis begins with these words: "In the beginning, God." John is saying the same thing with his introductory sentence: "In the beginning was the Word, and the Word was with God, and the Word was God." John makes it clear that the eternal Son of God was vitally involved in the creation of the world. John 1 echoes Genesis 1, showing that Jesus is God and showing that the Son of God's incarnation is as significant an event as the Father, Son, and Spirit's initial creation of the universe.

LIGHT AND DARKNESS. The first thing God creates is light (Gen. 1:3). Thus, human sin and all that is broken in the world is often described as "darkness." One of the plagues God brought upon Egypt was the plague of darkness: "Then the LORD said to Moses, 'Stretch out your hand toward heaven, that there may be darkness over the land of Egypt, a darkness to be felt'" (Ex. 10:21). John announces that, finally, with the arrival of Jesus, there is a true answer to the darkness in the world: "The true light, which gives light to everyone, was coming into the world" (1:9).

A BETTER MOSES. Long before sending Jesus to earth, God had been sending his people leaders such as prophets, judges, and kings to deliver them from their troubles. One of the greatest prophets God sent was Moses. God used Moses to deliver and shepherd the Israelites. Through Moses God gave his people the law. Yet Moses was an imperfect leader, a sinful man just like the men and women he was leading, who couldn't provide the deeper deliverance God's people needed. Moses couldn't accomplish the great act of grace that Jesus came to accomplish. "For the law was given through Moses; grace and truth came through Jesus Christ. No one has ever seen God; the only God, who is at the Father's side, he has made him known" (1:17–18). John 1 taps into this whole-Bible theme of men sent from God, showing us that Jesus is the ultimate man sent from God. Indeed, he is God himself.

Theological Soundings

DEITY OF CHRIST. Jesus is "the Word," and "the Word was with God, and the Word was God" (1:1). John wastes no time in telling us that Jesus is divine. The New Testament teaches that Jesus is included in the divine identity (Rom. 9:5; 1 Cor. 8:6; Col. 1:15–20; Heb. 1:3). While there are distinctions of persons within the one Godhead, Jesus Christ is as much God as God the Father and God the Holy Spirit.

TRINITY. The opening verses of John make clear that the Son of God—the Word—is also the same God who created the universe "in the beginning." Putting John 1 together with Genesis 1, we see here all three persons of the Trinity—Father, Son, and Spirit. John 1 plays a central role in revealing the doctrine of the Trinity. Broadly speaking, Christian theology teaches that the Father orchestrates salvation, the Son accomplishes salvation, and the Spirit applies salvation.

LAW AND GRACE. "For the law was given through Moses; grace and truth came through Jesus Christ" (1:17). Both the law[5] and grace are gifts from God. The Psalms are full of exclamations about the delight God's people take in his law. God gave his law to his people through Moses. The law revealed God's righteous character and the righteous requirements God made of his people. The law was and is a gift. But the law doesn't save. This verse from John teaches us that Jesus brings us a better revelation than Moses, for now in Jesus we receive a full picture of God's grace. The essence of grace is the news that God has met the requirements of the law for us through the perfect obedience of Jesus. It is only through this grace that we find the power to follow God's commands.

Personal Implications

Take time to reflect on the implications of John 1:1–18 for your own life today. Make notes below on the personal implications for your walk with the Lord of (1) the *Gospel Glimpses*, (2) the *Whole-Bible Connections*, (3) the *Theological Soundings*, and (4) this passage as a whole.

1. Gospel Glimpses

2. Whole-Bible Connections

17

3. Theological Soundings

4. John 1:1–18

As You Finish This Unit . . .

Take a moment now to ask for the Lord's blessing and help as you engage in this study of John. And take a moment also to look back through this unit of study, to reflect on a few key things that the Lord may be teaching you—and perhaps to highlight or underline these to review again in the future.

Definitions

[1] **Word** – Translation of the Greek term logos, literally meaning "word" or "logical principle." Equated with Jesus and God in John's Gospel (John 1:1–18). John is likely drawing upon the rich reservoir of meaning for the term both in Hellenistic thought and in first-century Judaism.

[2] **Incarnation** – Literally "(becoming) in flesh," it refers to God becoming a true human being in the person of Jesus of Nazareth.

[3] **Trinity** – The Godhead as it exists in three distinct persons: Father, Son, and Holy Spirit. There is one God, yet he is three persons; there are not three Gods, nor do the three persons merely represent different aspects or modes of a single God. While the term Trinity is not found in the Bible, the concept is repeatedly assumed and affirmed by the writers of Scripture (e.g., Matt. 28:19; Luke 1:35; 3:22; Gal. 4:6; 2 Thess. 2:13–14; Heb. 10:29).

[4] **Grace** – Unmerited favor, especially the free gift of salvation that God gives to believers through faith in Jesus Christ.

[5] **Law** – When spelled with an initial capital letter, "Law" refers to the first five books of the Bible. When spelled with an initial lowercased letter, "law" refers to the entire body of precepts set forth in those five books (also referred to as the "law of Moses"). The law contains numerous commands of God to his people, including the Ten Commandments and instructions regarding worship, sacrifice, and life in Israel.

WEEK 3:
JOHN THE BAPTIST
AND THE START OF
JESUS' MINISTRY

John 1:19–2:11

▲

The Place of the Passage

This introductory section of John's Gospel gives the account of the first week of Jesus' ministry. Jesus is declared to be "the Lamb of God" by John the Baptist; is followed by his first disciples; and performs his first sign, turning water into wine at the wedding at Cana. The first half of John's Gospel (1:19–12:50) highlights Jesus' messianic[1] identity through the many signs[2] that he performs.

The Big Picture

John 1:19–2:11 shows us that Jesus is the Lamb of God who takes away sins, calls disciples, and performs miraculous signs.

> ## Reflection and Discussion

This section of John contains three significant events in the early ministry of Jesus. Read John 1:19–2:11 and consider the following questions. (For further background, see the *ESV Study Bible*, pages 2020–2023; also available online at www.esvbible.org.)

1. The Testimony of John the Baptist (1:19–34)

The Pharisees[3] sent messengers to John to ask him one question: "Who are you?" (v. 19). Who are the three people John denies being, and how does John answer the Pharisees' question in verse 23?

The Christ, Elijah, the Prophet Isaiah

In verse 23 John the Baptist identifies himself with the prophet Isaiah's words. Read Isaiah 40:1–5. What is John the Baptist saying about who he is and who Jesus is?

a voice in the wilderness
Prepare the way of the Lord – Jesus

In John 1:29 John the Baptist declares who Jesus is and what Jesus does. Read Exodus 12:1–14. What connections do you see between this description of Jesus and the grace God showed his people in instituting the Passover ritual? What does John 1:29 say about what our broken world most needs?

Perfect. Without defect
Blood on doorposts

How would you explain the difference between the baptism[4] performed by John and the baptizing Jesus came to do?

[handwritten notes]

2. Jesus Calls the First Disciples (1:35–51)

What made the disciples[5] of John the Baptist decide to follow Jesus? What do the events of John 1:35–37 teach us about John the Baptist's ministry and about what all Christian ministry is ultimately meant to do?

[handwritten: Pointing to Jesus – Follow me. Call to repentance]

After leaving John the Baptist to follow Jesus, Andrew exclaimed to his brother, Peter, "'We have found the Messiah' (which means Christ)" (John 1:41). The Old Testament repeatedly speaks about the coming Messiah, the coming king or "anointed one." Isaiah 9:6–7 sums up many of these expectations. What does this Old Testament passage teach us to expect from the Messiah?

[handwritten: Born a child / Wonderful counselor]

In John 1:35–51 Jesus calls his first five disciples. As these disciples get to know Jesus, they say different things about him. List these various declarations. What is the significance of each of these declarations, and how do they deepen our understanding of who Jesus is and what he came to accomplish?

In John 1:51 Jesus alludes to Genesis 28:12 and Jacob's vision of a ladder between heaven and earth. Here Jesus reveals that *he* is the ladder that links heaven and earth. In today's culture, what "ladders" do people try to build between heaven and earth, attempting to bypass Jesus as Savior?

Good works

3. Jesus Performs His First Sign (2:1–11)

Jesus' first sign is turning water into wine, an act that saved a party from ending early. What do we learn about the ultimate purpose of what Jesus came to do, given that his first miracle kept a party going?

According to John 2:11, why did Jesus perform this first sign, and what was the effect of this sign?

Read through the following three sections on *Gospel Glimpses*, *Whole-Bible Connections*, and *Theological Soundings*. Then take time to reflect on the *Personal Implications* these sections may have for your walk with the Lord.

THE SIN REMOVER. John 1:29 summarizes who Jesus is and what Jesus does: "Behold, the Lamb of God, who takes away the sin of the world!" Jesus takes away sin. In the Old Testament the people of God traveled to the temple and made sacrifices, following elaborate instructions, in order to ensure that their sins were taken away. These sacrifices all pointed forward to the day that an ultimate sacrifice would be made for sin. Now, with the arrival of Jesus, we don't need to do anything to cover for our sins. Jesus covers for our sins. Jesus takes away the sin of the world. To have our sin totally taken away, all we must do is believe in him.

THE CALL OF DISCIPLESHIP. In John 1:35–51 Jesus summons five men to follow him, to be his disciples. Notice that Jesus initiates the relationship. And notice that Jesus doesn't ask his disciples to meet certain qualifications. To enter into a relationship with Jesus, only one thing is required: faith. As the Gospel accounts all testify, Jesus' original band of disciples didn't have it all together—they routinely sinned, failed, and made a mess of things. Yet Jesus loved them. It was Jesus who first called them to follow him. This passage makes clear that the deciding factor in this relationship is Jesus and his grace, not us and our qualifications. In fact, the only way to have a relationship with Jesus is to know that you do not qualify!

A LADDER TO HEAVEN. Recalling events and imagery from Jacob's dream (Genesis 28), Jesus tells his first disciples of the great things they will see from him: "Truly, truly, I say to you, you will see heaven opened, and the angels of God ascending and descending on the Son of Man" (John 1:51). Ever since man's relationship with God was severed in the garden of Eden, we've been trying to bridge the gap between heaven and earth, trying to construct a ladder from earth to heaven. Here Jesus proclaims that no such ladder can be built—that we need a ladder that moves from heaven to earth, a ladder that only God can provide. Jesus states that he is this ladder; he has come from heaven to earth to be the ladder men and women need in order to enter back into a relationship with the God of heaven and earth. This ladder stands on grace, not works. In Jesus, God has moved toward us, providing access to heaven for sinners. Faith in Jesus takes us to the top of the ladder.

LAMB OF GOD. Jesus, by his perfectly righteous life, sacrificial death on the cross, and victorious resurrection from the grave, fulfills all the symbolism of the Passover lamb and other Old Testament sacrifices. As the apostle Paul states, "Christ, our Passover lamb, has been sacrificed" (1 Cor. 5:7). In the Old Testament, deliverance through the shed blood of an animal, most notably the Passover lamb, prefigured the coming of Jesus as the Lamb of God who once and for all obtained salvation for God's people. John, the author of this Gospel, continues to speak of Jesus in this way in the final book of the Bible, Revelation, as he depicts Jesus as the apocalyptic warrior Lamb who brings final judgment to the world (Rev. 5:6–13; 7:17; 21:22–23; 22:1–3).

MIRACLES. Throughout Scripture, whenever God is up to something big and new, his work is accompanied by miracles. We see this most notably in God's creation of the universe (Genesis 1–2), the exodus from Egypt (Exodus 1–12), and God's reforming work through the prophets Elijah and Elisha (1 and 2 Kings). In John, immediately after calling his first disciples, Jesus performs a miracle (sign), turning water into wine. As John's Gospel progresses, so do the miracles of Jesus—the miracles become more and more significant. Consistent with the story line of Scripture, the many miracles in Jesus' ministry are a sign that a new epoch has arrived in God's dealings with his people.

Theological Soundings

MESSIAH. Jesus' identity as the long-awaited Messiah is clearly proclaimed in this section of John. Consider the diversity of declarations made about Jesus in this section. John the Baptist: "Behold, the Lamb of God, who takes away the sin of the world!" (1:29) and "I have seen and have borne witness that this is the Son of God" (1:34). Andrew: "'We have found the Messiah' (which means Christ)" (1:41). Philip: "We have found him of whom Moses in the Law and also the prophets wrote, Jesus of Nazareth, the son of Joseph" (1:45). Nathanael: "Rabbi, you are the Son of God! You are the King of Israel!" (1:49). And Jesus himself reveals his messianic identity: "Truly, truly, I say to you, you will see heaven opened, and the angels of God ascending and descending on the Son of Man" (1:51).

HOLY SPIRIT. The third person of the Trinity shows up in this section of John, as John the Baptist testifies: "I saw the Spirit descend from heaven like a dove, and it remained on him [Jesus]" (1:32). Reminiscent of the presence and activity of the Spirit in the opening sentences of Genesis, here we see the Holy Spirit fill and remain upon Jesus. This was a messianic anointing, empowering him to begin his ministry of discipleship, miracles, teaching, and suffering. We see in the ministry of Jesus what we see throughout the Bible: the Holy Spirit is the one who empowers ministry.

> ## Personal Implications

Take time to reflect on the implications of John 1:19–2:11 for your own life today. Make notes below on the personal implications for your walk with the Lord of (1) the *Gospel Glimpses*, (2) the *Whole-Bible Connections*, (3) the *Theological Soundings*, and (4) this passage as a whole.

1. Gospel Glimpses

2. Whole-Bible Connections

3. Theological Soundings

4. John 1:19–2:11

> ### As You Finish This Unit . . .

Take a moment now to ask for the Lord's blessing and help as you engage in this study of John. And take a moment also to look back through this unit of study, to reflect on a few key things that the Lord may be teaching you—and perhaps to highlight or underline these to review again in the future.

Definitions

[1] **Messiah** – Transliteration of a Hebrew word meaning "anointed one," the equivalent of the Greek word Christ. Originally applied to anyone specially designated for a particular role, such as king or priest. Jesus himself affirmed that he was the Messiah, sent from God (Matt. 16:16–17).

[2] **Signs** – Miracles that attest to Jesus' identity as Messiah and Son of God and lead unbelievers to faith.

[3] **Pharisee** – A member of a popular religious/political party in NT times characterized by strict adherence to the law of Moses and also to extrabiblical Jewish traditions. The Pharisees were frequently criticized by Jesus for their legalistic and hypocritical practices. The apostle Paul was a zealous Pharisee prior to his conversion.

[4] **Baptism** – Literally "to immerse" or "to wash." Refers to the Christian practice of immersing a new believer in water as an outward sign of the inward reality of regeneration. This regeneration is the work of the Holy Spirit (see John 3:5, 8; Titus 3:5) and may be received only by grace through faith (see Eph. 2:8). Considerable disagreement exists as to method of baptism (e.g., pouring or sprinkling versus immersion) and who may be baptized (e.g., believers and their infant children versus believers only).

[5] **Disciple** – Any person who submits to the teachings of another. In the NT, refers to those who submitted themselves to the teaching of Jesus, especially those who traveled with him during his earthly ministry.

WEEK 4:
JESUS' EXPANDING
MINISTRY

John 2:12–4:54

▲

The Place of the Passage

In this section of John, Jesus' Jerusalem ministry begins with the clearing of the temple.[1] Jesus then has three major encounters with three very different types of people: Nicodemus, a representative of the Jewish religious establishment; a Samaritan woman; and a Gentile official. The main effect of these chapters is to reveal more of who Jesus is and to highlight the expansive extent of what Jesus came to do.

The Big Picture

John 2:12–4:54 shows that there is only one way to God and eternal life: through belief in Jesus.

> ## Reflection and Discussion

Read through the complete passage for this study, John 2:12–4:54. Then review the four sections listed below and write your notes on the following questions. (For further background, see the *ESV Study Bible*, pages 2023–2030; also available online at www.esvbible.org.)

1. Jesus Cleanses the Temple (2:12–25)

Jesus' first major confrontation with the Jewish leaders in John's Gospel occurs as Jesus clears the Jerusalem temple during the Jewish Passover. Why did Jesus clear the temple, in light of the true purpose of the temple? What does this scene teach us about Jesus?

They were selling animals for sacrifice

making it a marketplace

After cleansing the temple, Jesus converses with the Jewish leaders and makes a statement about his approaching death and resurrection, as well as about his identity as the true and better temple for God's people. Skim through Solomon's prayer of dedication for the temple (2 Chron. 6:12–42). In what ways do you see Jesus as the ultimate answer to this prayer?

2. Jesus Teaches a Jew about Salvation (3:1–36)

Nicodemus is a Pharisee, a respected scholar among the Jews, who approaches Jesus "by night." Why might Nicodemus have approached Jesus at night? How and why does Jesus steer the conversation in the direction that he does?

Might be seen by day.

According to John 3:3, what must happen for someone to see the kingdom of God? According to 3:4–8, what must happen for someone to be born again?[2]

Born again
Born of water + the Spirit

John 3:16 is probably the most well known verse in the Bible. If this were the only verse we had, what would we know about God and salvation?[3]

God loved the world.
Gave His only Son to die for the sins of the world

3. Jesus Teaches a Samaritan about Salvation (4:1–45)

In this scene Jesus does something scandalous for a first-century Jewish rabbi: he enters into compassionate dialogue with a Samaritan woman with a questionable past. Jesus is always doing things like this, crossing boundaries to show that God's grace is not limited to a certain type of person. According to Jesus, salvation is for sinners. In other words, salvation is for everyone. What does this scene teach us about what Jesus is like, and what does it teach us about salvation?

loving God
Salvation for sinners — everyone

What does the woman do after her encounter with Jesus? What do we learn from this?

Tells others — Many believed

4. Ministry by Deed (4:46–54)

John has shown Jesus bringing the gospel to a respected Jewish teacher (John 3:1–21), then to an outcast Samaritan woman (4:1–42), and now to an official working for the Roman government (4:46–54). This drives home the truth that the good news of God's grace is available for all types of people, to everyone in the world. Reflecting on these three different people, consider how they each respond to Jesus. What do their responses to Jesus teach us about how we should respond to the Son of God?

How did Jesus heal the official's son? What is John communicating to us about the power of Jesus' words?

J. said Go your son lives
words powerful,

Read through the following three sections on *Gospel Glimpses*, *Whole-Bible Connections*, and *Theological Soundings*. Then take time to reflect on the *Personal Implications* these sections may have for your walk with the Lord.

Gospel Glimpses

RESURRECTION POWER. Foreshadowing his own death and resurrection, Jesus told the religious leaders, "Destroy this temple, and in three days I will raise it up" (John 2:19). This is what Jesus can do with death: undo it. There is no life so broken that Jesus cannot fix it. Jesus turns spiritually dead people into living people. His resurrection power works best in graveyards!

NEW BIRTH. According to John 3, salvation comes not fundamentally through a human decision or fresh resolve but by being "born again." This requirement Jesus issues—"You must be born again" (3:7)—cannot be performed by men or women themselves any more than was their first, physical birth. The Spirit of God must accomplish this. God himself must grant and perform the miracle of new birth. According to John 3, salvation is not at its core mental assent to a new doctrine or resolution to live differently. Salvation comes, most fundamentally, through the miracle of new birth, whereby our hearts are set free to put our trust in Jesus.

COSTLY LOVE. John 3:16 is surely the most famous verse in the Bible. It is famous for good reason—this sentence powerfully summarizes the gospel message. The heart of this message is costly love. God's love for the world was so great that he endured the loss of his only Son in order to save us. The Son of God lost his life in order that we might gain life. God's love is free for us, but it cost him dearly.

Whole-Bible Connections

THE TRUE TEMPLE. After clearing the temple, Jesus issues a bold claim: "Destroy this temple, and in three days I will raise it up" (John 2:19). For centuries the Jerusalem temple had stood as the meeting place between God and man—the physical place where heaven and earth met, atonement was made for sins, and God communed with his people. Here Jesus declares that he is the true temple, the true meeting place for God and man. Jesus states that after being destroyed by death, he would come back from death. And this, indeed, is what Jesus did—proving that he is the true and better temple, the temple that cannot be destroyed.

MISSIONARY GOD. From Genesis 1:1 on through Revelation 22:21, God reveals himself as a missionary God. God is constantly engaged in missionary activity, making himself known to people who are far from him. God initiated his missionary plan with Abraham, stating that through his offspring "all the families of the earth shall be blessed" (Genesis 12:3). Jesus, the true and final offspring of Abraham (Gal. 3:16), demonstrates God's missionary heart here in John 3 and 4. He brings the message of salvation to three different kinds of people who desperately need to know God: a Jewish leader, an outcast Samaritan woman, and a Gentile official. Jesus brings to a climax God's missionary activity, for in Jesus God became flesh in order to make himself known to a lost world.

Theological Soundings

GOD'S INITIATIVE. Our relationship with God starts with God, not with us. God always makes the first move in establishing a saving relationship with his people. John 3 states that for a person to know God, God must first take action as he grants "new birth." In the Old Testament we see that people entered into a relationship with God only because God initiated it, because God called them. And in the New Testament we see the same thing—a relationship with God starts with God. As John puts it in one of his letters, "We love because he first loved us" (1 John 4:19).

THE WORD OF GOD. God's word is powerful. In Genesis 1 God creates the universe through his words: "And God said, 'Let there be light,' and there was light" (Gen. 1:3). Throughout the Old Testament God saves people, destroys nations, and performs miracles, all through his word. And throughout the New Testament it is through the word of God that events of significance happen. Jesus, God in the flesh, heals an official's son simply through speaking words: "Go; your son will live" (John 4:50). As Jesus said to Satan, quoting

Deuteronomy, "Man shall not live by bread alone, but by every word that comes from the mouth of God" (Matt. 4:4). Indeed, Jesus himself *is* the final "Word" of God (John 1:1)—Jesus and his saving work is what God has to say to the world.

Personal Implications

Take time to reflect on the implications of John 2:12–4:54 for your own life today. Make notes below on the personal implications for your walk with the Lord of (1) the *Gospel Glimpses*, (2) the *Whole-Bible Connections*, (3) the *Theological Soundings*, and (4) this passage as a whole.

1. Gospel Glimpses

The Spirit of God grants the miracle of salvation — new birth

2. Whole-Bible Connections

Jesus the true temple. Meeting of God and men.

3. Theological Soundings

Our Relationship with God starts with God

4. John 2:12–4:54

As You Finish This Unit . . .

Take a moment now to ask for the Lord's blessing and help as you engage in this study of John. And take a moment also to look back through this unit of study, to reflect on a few key things that the Lord may be teaching you—and perhaps to highlight or underline these to review again in the future.

Definitions

[1] **Temple** – A place set aside as holy because of God's presence there. Solomon built the first temple of the Lord in Jerusalem, to replace the portable tabernacle. This temple was later destroyed by the Babylonians, rebuilt, and destroyed again by the Romans.

[2] **Born again** – A phrase used by Jesus in John 3 to describe how a person enters the kingdom of heaven. Natural birth is not sufficient. Instead, through the work of the Holy Spirit and the grace of God, a person must experience a second, spiritual birth, in which he or she becomes a new person in Christ.

[3] **Salvation** – Deliverance from the eternal consequences of sin. Jesus' death and resurrection purchased eternal salvation for believers (Rom. 1:16).

WEEK 5:
MORE SIGNS AMID
MOUNTING JEWISH
OPPOSITION

John 5:1–10:42

▲

> ## The Place of the Passage

At this juncture in John, the conflict escalates between Jesus and the Jewish leaders. Along the way, Jesus defends his ministry and reveals more about the aims of his mission. In his defense, Jesus further reveals his identity, performs more signs, and cites several major witnesses on his behalf.

> ## The Big Picture

In John 5:1–10:42 Jesus explicitly declares that he is God, the second person of the Trinity, and that he has authority over all things.

▶ Reflection and Discussion

Read through the complete passage for this study, John 5:1–10:42. Then review the three sections below and write your notes on the questions concerning this phase of escalating conflict and revelation in Jesus' ministry. (For further background, see the *ESV Study Bible*, pages 2030–2045; also available online at www.esvbible.org.)

1. Jesus Is God (5:1–6:71)

According to John 5:18, why were the Jews[1] seeking to kill Jesus?

Broken sabbath rule?

Review John 5. Make a list of everything this passage teaches us about God the Father, about God the Son, and about the relationship God the Father and God the Son enjoy.

Father & son one   *Both give life*

During Passover,[2] Jesus turns five loaves and two fish into a feast for thousands. What does this sign teach us about Jesus? What Old Testament account might form the background to this miracle? What does the aftermath of this miracle (John 6:22–71) teach us about the human heart and mankind's ultimate need?

What does Jesus mean when he says, "I am the bread of life" (John 6:35)?

Essential to life

2. Jesus Is the Christ (7:1–8:59)

Read Proverbs 4:23 and Isaiah 58:11. Jesus is likely referring to these two Old Testament passages when he likens himself and the work of the Holy Spirit[3] to "rivers of living water" (John 7:37–39). When John says, "for as yet the Spirit had not been given" (7:39), he doesn't mean that there was no work of the Holy Spirit in the world prior to Jesus' resurrection. After all, the opening page of our Bible testifies to the Spirit's activity in the world (Gen. 1:2), as do several more Old Testament passages. John is simply stating that the Holy Spirit had not yet been given in the full and powerful sense as promised in Joel 2:28–29, and as later experienced on the day of Pentecost (Acts 2:1–11). How do these supporting passages from Joel and Acts help illuminate John 7:37–39?

The earliest manuscripts of the Gospel of John do not contain John 7:53–8:11. It seems best to view the story as something that happened during Jesus' ministry but was not an original part of what John wrote. What does this scene teach us about how Jesus treats sinners who are aware of their sin and how Jesus treats sinners who are unaware of their sin?

3. Jesus Is One with the Father (9:1–10:42)

In John 9:2 Jesus' disciples ask an important question about suffering. How does Jesus answer their question? What do you think of this answer, and how does it help us make sense out of the suffering we see and experience?

As John's Gospel progresses, Jesus more explicitly reveals his identity and his mission. Review John 10:22–42. What do we learn here about who Jesus is and what he came to do?

Read through the following three sections on *Gospel Glimpses*, *Whole-Bible Connections*, and *Theological Soundings*. Then take time to reflect on the *Personal Implications* these sections may have for your walk with the Lord.

Gospel Glimpses

THE POWER OF JESUS. John 5:1–17 narrates Jesus' encounter with a man who had been an "invalid" (the Greek term for a "disabled" condition) for thirty-eight years. This man had stationed himself near a pool thought to have healing powers. Jesus speaks a sentence to him, and he is instantly healed: "Jesus said to him, 'Get up, take up your bed, and walk.' And at once the man was healed" (John 5:8–9). Thirty-eight years of disability are shed simply through the voice of Jesus. No matter the extent of sin or sickness in someone's life, Jesus can completely transform him or her through his power. In fact, the only people Jesus works with to save and change are sick and sinful people.

THE ANSWER. Throughout this section of John, Jesus constantly reveals himself as the ultimate answer to the world's problems. Jesus is the "bread of life" (John 6) who relieves our true hunger, a hunger that food cannot fix. Jesus offers "living water" (John 7) that quenches the thirst we can't quench on our own. Jesus is the "light of the world" (John 8) who takes away the darkness that engulfs us. And Jesus is the "good shepherd" (John 10) who tenderly cares for us. And unlike bread and water, it requires no money or effort to know Jesus. All we need to do is admit our hunger and ask for this free "bread of life."

TWO TYPES OF SINNERS. Though the earliest manuscripts of the Gospel of John do not include John 7:53–8:11, this story reveals an important distinction that shows up throughout the Bible: there are two types of sinners. The woman caught in adultery is a sinner, and she knows it. Thus, Jesus immediately forgives the woman. The scribes and Pharisees are sinners, but they don't know it. Thus, Jesus confronts them with the truth of their sin. For grace to be enjoyed and received, one must first see one's own sin and need for grace.

Whole-Bible Connections

ONE BIG STORY. Jesus defends his divine identity and ministry by appealing to Moses, saying, "If you believed Moses, you would believe me; for he wrote of me" (John 5:46). This is one of the many places where Jesus argues that the Old Testament Scriptures are about him, that the Bible tells one big story about him. Jesus teaches us that the point of the Old Testament is to point to him—the Son of God who has come to take away the sins of the world.

DO NOT BE AFRAID. The command that appears most often in the Old Testament is the simple imperative "Do not be afraid," or "Fear not." The Old Testament is filled with God's call not to be afraid. This command reaches a climax with the arrival of the Son of God. In the midst of a storm, while walking on water, Jesus says to his frightened disciples, "It is I; do not be afraid" (John 6:20). To come face-to-face with Jesus is to come face-to-face with God, and in this scene we see why God has filled the Scriptures with the attractive command to abandon fear: for God himself has left heaven to approach us in the midst of our storm and bring us safely back to shore. He does this ultimately through the cross of his own dear Son.

THE GOOD SHEPHERD. In John 10:11 Jesus announces, "I am the good shepherd. The good shepherd lays down his life for the sheep." With these two sentences Jesus brings to a climax the longings of God's people. "God . . . has been my shepherd all my life long," said Jacob (Gen. 48:15). "The LORD is my shepherd," wrote David (Ps. 23:1). God "will tend his flock like a shepherd," prophesied Isaiah (Isa. 40:11). Over time, these ancient descriptions of God as the true shepherd fueled the longing for a shepherd-leader, a shepherd-king, a

Messiah, who would lead God's sheep in wisdom and restoration—"But you, O Bethlehem Ephrathah, who are too little to be among the clans of Judah, from you shall come forth for me one who is to be ruler in Israel, whose coming forth is from of old, from ancient days. . . . And he shall stand and shepherd his flock in the strength of the LORD" (Mic. 5:2, 4; note also Num. 27:16–17; Jer. 3:15; 23:4). In this section of John—the feeding of the five thousand, the healing of the sick, the forgiving of sinners, and the claim to be "the good shepherd"—we see Jesus fulfilling this ancient longing and promise.

Theological Soundings

THE AUTHORITY OF SCRIPTURE. Jesus repeatedly defends his ministry throughout this section of John by appealing to Scripture. Jesus quotes the Old Testament, most notably in reference to Moses and Abraham, to validate his identity and ministry. For Jesus, the highest appeal one can make is to the Scriptures, for the Scriptures are God's authoritative Word. Among the many arguments to be made for the authority of Scripture, the greatest argument is that Jesus himself treated holy Scripture as authoritative and submitted his life to it.

THE CALL OF GOD. In John's Gospel, Jesus repeatedly states that a relationship with God begins with God's initiative. To a crowd Jesus says, "No one can come to me unless the Father who sent me draws him" (John 6:44). Jesus' words are consistent with the entire witness of the Bible—humans cannot self-generate a relationship with God. God must first call a person into relationship with himself. We see this first in Genesis 12, when God calls Abram out of the crowd and into a relationship with himself. Along with Jesus, the apostle Paul often highlighted this truth.

Personal Implications

Take time to reflect on the implications of John 5:1–10:42 for your own life today. Make notes below on the personal implications for your walk with the Lord of (1) the *Gospel Glimpses*, (2) the *Whole-Bible Connections*, (3) the *Theological Soundings*, and (4) this passage as a whole.

1. Gospel Glimpses

2. Whole-Bible Connections

3. Theological Soundings

4. John 5:1–10:42

As You Finish This Unit . . .

Take a moment now to ask for the Lord's blessing and help as you engage in this study of John. And take a moment also to look back through this unit of study, to reflect on a few key things that the Lord may be teaching you—and perhaps to highlight or underline these to review again in the future.

Definitions

[1] **Jew** – A person belonging to one of the tribes of Israel. The term, derived from the word "Judah/Judean," came into general usage around the time of the Babylonian exile (c. 586–516 BC). It is sometimes clear that when John refers to "the Jews," he has in mind particularly the Jewish leaders, the Pharisees and Sadducees.

[2] **Passover** – An annual Israelite festival commemorating God's final plague on the Egyptians, which led to the exodus. In this final plague, the Lord "passed over" the houses of those who spread the blood of a lamb on the doorposts and lintel of their homes (Exodus 12). Those who did not obey this command suffered the death of their firstborn.

[3] **Holy Spirit** – One of the persons of the Trinity, and thus fully God. The Bible mentions several roles of the Holy Spirit, including convicting people of sin, bringing them to conversion, indwelling them and empowering them to live in righteousness and faithfulness, supporting them in times of trial, and enabling them to understand the Scriptures. The Holy Spirit inspired the writers of Scripture, guiding them to record the very words of God. The Holy Spirit was uniquely active in Jesus' life and ministry on earth (e.g., 1:32–34; Luke 3:22).

WEEK 6:
THE FINAL PASSOVER:
THE ULTIMATE SIGN

John 11:1–12:19

▲

The Place of the Passage

This is a pivotal section in John's Gospel. Everything changes as Jesus performs his final and ultimate "sign" in this Gospel, raising a man from the dead. This incredible miracle (recorded only by John) foreshadows Jesus' own resurrection[1] and significantly escalates Jesus' conflict with the Jewish leaders. The raising of a man from the dead triggers the Jewish leaders' determination to have Jesus arrested and put to death.

The Big Picture

In John 11:1–12:19 Jesus raises a man from the dead, prefiguring his own death and resurrection and stirring the Jewish leaders to pursue his arrest and death.

▶ Reflection and Discussion

Read through the complete passage for this study, John 11:1–12:19. Then review the questions below and write your notes on them concerning this phase of Jesus' ministry. (For further background, see the *ESV Study Bible*, pages 2045–2048; also available online at www.esvbible.org.)

Jesus' ministry was full of friendship. It is clear that Jesus had a unique and special relationship with three of his disciples: Peter, James, and John. Jesus appears to also have a strong bond of friendship with the characters featured in John 11—Lazarus, Mary, and Martha: "Now Jesus loved Martha and her sister and Lazarus" (John 11:5). How does this expand your portrait of Jesus? What do you make of the fact that ordinary people can have a friendship with the Son of God?

human
accessible
human
friend

In 11:4 Jesus teaches two life-changing truths. First, Jesus knows the future. Second, God has bigger purposes for human suffering than humans are able to see. How could these statements by Jesus transform your approach to life's difficulties?

Trust in God - wait for him

John states that after Jesus heard Lazarus was ill, "he stayed two days longer in the place where he was" (11:6). Instead of immediately going to Lazarus, Jesus waits. How does John 11:5 and the rest of John chapter 11 further clarify why Jesus didn't immediately go to Lazarus?

According to John 11:14–15, why is Jesus glad that he wasn't there when Lazarus died? What do these two verses, along with 11:4, teach us about the point of this sign that Jesus is performing?

Before raising Lazarus, Jesus engages with Lazarus's sisters, Martha and Mary. Jesus interacts with Martha and Mary very differently. How does Jesus respond to Martha, and how does he respond to Mary? What does this teach us about Jesus?

What does Jesus do immediately before raising Lazarus from the dead? How does Jesus raise Lazarus from the dead? What can we learn from this scene about the power of prayer and the power of God's voice?

Prays
Word

After raising Lazarus, the opposition against Jesus intensifies. "So from that day on they made plans to put him to death" (John 11:53). Caiaphas, the high priest, was involved in the discussions about whether or not to pursue Jesus' death. In 11:49–50, how does Caiaphas preach the gospel without knowing it?

After raising Lazarus from the dead, Jesus enjoys a special dinner with Lazarus and others (John 12:1–8). Judas expresses disappointment when Mary breaks the nard over Jesus' feet. How does Jesus respond to Judas, and what is surprising about this response?

Why did the chief priests decide that they also wanted to put Lazarus to death? See John 12:11 and 11:48.

Jesus enters Jerusalem for the Passover, seated on a donkey and hailed by the people. This scene draws on a prophecy in Zechariah. Read Zechariah 9:9–17 to get a sense for the expectations that were in people's minds as their "King of Israel"[2] entered Jerusalem. Less than a week later, how did the people treat Jesus (see John 19:14–16)?

Read through the following three sections on *Gospel Glimpses*, *Whole-Bible Connections*, and *Theological Soundings*. Then take time to reflect on the *Personal Implications* this passage from John may have for your walk with the Lord.

Gospel Glimpses

DEATH BEFORE LIFE. Jesus repeatedly teaches that for something to really live, it must first die: "Truly, truly I say to you, unless a grain of wheat falls into the earth and dies, it remains alone; but if it dies, it bears much fruit" (John 12:24). The gospel works this way. To experience new life in Christ, one must first die to his or her old life. Lazarus's story illustrates this. Jesus didn't want to deal with Lazarus's sickness; he wanted to deal with Lazarus's death. Jesus' resurrection power shows up in tombs, not hospital beds. John 11 should be read alongside John 3, where Jesus teaches Nicodemus the need to be "born again." Following Jesus isn't easy. We do not simply add Jesus to our existing life. Instead, Jesus calls men and women to die to their old life so that he can give us new life—resurrection life.

PERSONAL GRACE. Before handling Lazarus's death, Jesus first interacts with Lazarus's sisters, Martha and Mary. Jesus deals with the two grieving sisters very differently. Jesus gave Martha teaching, but he gave Mary his tears. Jesus knew Martha. He knew that she needed teaching—she needed to hear Jesus say, "I am the resurrection and the life. Whoever believes in me, though he die, yet shall he live" (John 11:25). Mary needed something different—she needed Jesus' tender sympathy (John 11:35). This is how Jesus deals with people. He knows us. He knows our story, our personality, our pain, and our unique needs. Jesus doesn't deal with us generically. He deals with us in a wonderfully personal way.

47

Whole-Bible Connections

PROPHECY FULFILLED. The Old Testament spoke of Israel's Messiah, who would one day enter Jerusalem mounted on a donkey (Zech. 9:9; Ps. 118:25–26). Waving palm branches and shouting messages of acclaim, the people expected Jesus to take charge and bring them political deliverance from their enemies, the Romans. The people, however, had not read their Hebrew Scriptures closely enough. The prophet Isaiah wrote that the Messiah would be a suffering servant, who would lay down his life in order to bring life to his people, rescuing them from their deeper problem: sin. "But he was pierced for our transgressions; he was crushed for our iniquities; upon him was the chastisement that brought us peace, and with his wounds we are healed" (Isa. 53:5).

Theological Soundings

GOD'S TIMING. When Jesus heard that Lazarus was ill, "he stayed two days longer in the place where he was" (John 11:6). Instead of going to Lazarus immediately, Jesus waited. Why did Jesus wait? John 11:5 tells us it was because of love. Reading John 11:5 and John 11:6 together, we see that it was because of his great love for Lazarus that Jesus waited to help Lazarus. This is how God works. God's timing is different from our timing. He sees things that we can't see. He has plans that we do not yet understand. In the case of Lazarus, Jesus waited in order to do a greater work in and through Lazarus's life—the greatest sign Jesus had yet performed in John's Gospel. God's timing is never off. He always knows what he is doing.

RESURRECTION. The Christian worldview teaches something unique: the bodily resurrection of the dead. Jesus raised Lazarus from the dead, yet Lazarus would later die again. What Jesus teaches, however, is that he is "the resurrection and the life. Whoever believes in me, though he die, yet shall he live, and everyone who lives and believes in me shall never die" (John 11:25–26). Jesus' teaching here expands upon teaching found throughout the Bible that both the righteous and the wicked will be resurrected, the righteous to eternal life and the wicked to judgment.

Personal Implications

Take time to reflect on the implications of John 11:1–12:19 for your own life today. Make notes below on the personal implications for your walk with the Lord of (1) the *Gospel Glimpses*, (2) the *Whole-Bible Connections*, (3) the *Theological Soundings*, and (4) this passage as a whole.

1. Gospel Glimpses

2. Whole-Bible Connections

3. Theological Soundings

4. John 11:1–12:19

As You Finish This Unit . . .

Take a moment now to ask for the Lord's blessing and help as you engage in this study of John. And take a moment also to look back through this unit of study, to reflect on a few key things that the Lord may be teaching you—and perhaps to highlight or underline these to review again in the future.

Definitions

[1] **Resurrection** – The impartation of new, eternal life to a dead person at the end of time (or in the case of Jesus, on the third day after his death). This new life is not a mere resuscitation of the body (as in the case of Lazarus; John 11:1–44), but a transformation of the body to an eternal state (1 Cor. 15:35–58). Both the righteous and the wicked will be resurrected, the former to eternal life and the latter to judgment (John 5:29).

[2] **Israel** – Originally, another name given to Jacob (Gen. 32:28). Later applied to the nation formed by his descendants, then to the ten northern tribes of that nation, who rejected the anointed king and formed their own nation. In the NT, the name is applied to the church as the spiritual descendants of Abraham (Gal. 6:16).

WEEK 7:
THE MESSIAH'S
DEATH AT HAND

John 12:20–50

▲

The Place of this Passage

John 12:20–50 brings to a close the first major part of John's Gospel, which has narrated Jesus' mission to the Jews. With the arrival of some Greeks seeking Jesus, Jesus announces the climax of his mission, his substitutionary[1] death, which is for both Jews and Gentiles. The remainder of John's Gospel unfolds Jesus' final meal with his disciples, his death, and his resurrection.

The Big Picture

In John 12:20–50 Jesus announces his approaching death and reveals the broad extent of his mission—to reconcile both Jews and Gentiles to God.

Reflection and Discussion

Read through the complete passage for this study, John 12:20–50. Then review the questions below and write your notes on them concerning this phase of Jesus' ministry. (For further background, see the *ESV Study Bible*, pages 2048–2050; also available online at www.esvbible.org.)

This section of John begins with some Greeks who have come to Jerusalem to worship at the Jewish festival. "Greeks" refers to Gentiles, not necessarily people from Greece. What is the difference between a Jew and a Gentile? From what you know of the Bible and first-century history, write out a definition for the word *Jew*, and for the word *Gentile*. How did they view one another?

Jew - an adherent of Judaism   Abraham
Gentiles anyone not Jewish

/ God   Many - Gentiles

These Gentiles approach Jesus' disciple Philip, saying, "Sir, we wish to see Jesus" (John 12:21). Why do you think these Gentiles wished to see Jesus?

miracles ?

Jesus gives an interesting response to the Greeks' desire to see him (John 12:23–26). What is Jesus' response? How do you make sense of it?

The hour has come for the son to be glorified

Jesus says, "The hour has come for the Son of Man[2] to be glorified" (John 12:23). He then gives an illustration about a grain of wheat. How does this sentence about a grain of wheat illustrate what Jesus came to accomplish with his life, and how does it illustrate what must happen in the lives of all who follow Jesus?

Je said die but new life is given

John 12:28 gives one of three instances in Jesus' earthly ministry where a heavenly voice attests to his identity. Read Matthew 3:17 and 17:5 to note the other two instances. What is the significance of these three instances? In other words, why at these three junctures does a heavenly voice validate Jesus' identity and mission? How does John 12:30 add to the discussion?

Baptism + Transfiguration

for your benefit

John 12:31 is an important verse: "Now is the judgment of this world; now will the ruler of this world be cast out." The "ruler of this world" is Satan,[3] and Jesus states that his death on the cross will result in defeat for Satan. Read Hebrews 2:14–15 and Colossians 2:13–15. How do these two passages further illuminate what Jesus says here in John?

He shared humanity - because Son of God

Made alive thru Christ

Just as he did with the Greeks, Jesus again responds to a query with an interesting answer. How does Jesus reply to the crowd's questions in John 12:34? What is Jesus saying here? Jesus has used similar phrasing in John 8:12, 9:4, and 11:9–10. How do these passages add color to what Jesus is saying here?

Who is Son of Man

Light
Do His work while it is day

John 12:37 is startling. After all that Jesus has said and done, how have the people responded to him? John quotes the prophet Isaiah to explain what is going on. How do these passages from Isaiah explain the people's reaction to Jesus?

Didn't believe him

According to John 12:47, why did Jesus come to the world?

To save it.

Believe in J.

If you believe in J belief in J
same as judges them.
"Light of the world"

Read through the following three sections on *Gospel Glimpses*, *Whole-Bible Connections*, and *Theological Soundings*. Then take time to reflect on the *Personal Implications* these sections may have for your walk with the Lord.

Gospel Glimpses

HATING LIFE TO GAIN LIFE. At first glance, Jesus' words in John 12:25 sound demanding and difficult: "Whoever loves his life loses it, and whoever hates his life in this world will keep it for eternal life." As difficult as these words are, however, they are even more profoundly filled with grace. Jesus is showing us the way to true life. He is offering freedom. Jesus invites us to love and trust him more than we love and trust ourselves, for true life—eternal life—is found when we let go of our life and trust God to take care of us and direct us. The issue is whom we declare as the "god" of our life. If we continue to operate as god of our own life, we will eventually lose our life, for we were never meant to run our own lives and we are incapable of doing so. But if we take ourselves off the throne and declare that God truly is sovereign over our life and the universe, we will discover the true and eternal life that God means for us to enjoy. As Jesus says in Matthew 10:39, "Whoever finds his life will lose it, and whoever loses his life for my sake will find it."

FREED FROM SLAVERY. John 12 reports that some people began to believe in Jesus, but they kept this belief private because of fear. These people were afraid of being "put out of the synagogue" (John 12:42), an important place of social and communal standing at the time. John highlights the root of their fear: "for they loved the glory that comes from man more than the glory that comes from God" (John 12:43). This sentence describes us. By nature we all love the glory, approval, and recognition that people bestow on us. In fact, we love it so much that we're enslaved to it—we won't do anything that would compromise this glory. Jesus came to set us free from this miserable slavery. He knows that our problem isn't merely that we commit sins; our problem is that sin runs so deep in our hearts that we will worship anything other than God. We are enslaved to these false masters. Jesus is teaching us here how deep our slavery runs—so deep that it cost Jesus his life to set us free.

Whole-Bible Connections

GOD OF THE NATIONS. Long ago, in Genesis 12, God called a man named Abram (Abraham) into a relationship with him. God told Abraham that he would use him and his descendants to "be a blessing" (Gen. 12:2-3) to the nations. Jesus, a descendant of Abraham, brings to a climax God's calling on Abraham's life. Here in John 12 we see Gentiles flocking to Jesus, saying, "Sir, we wish to see Jesus" (John 12:21). God's long-promised plan reached a new level of fulfillment as Jesus came to earth and exercised his ministry among both Jews and Gentiles. After Jesus' resurrection and ascension, the book of Acts further documents that God is a God of the nations as the gospel spreads from Jerusalem out to the ends of the earth, reaching many different cities, nations, and types of people. Today, the mission continues as the God of the nations uses us to reach new people groups with the gospel of Jesus Christ.

VISION AND BLINDNESS. John 12:38–41 picks up on a major theme that appears throughout the Bible: spiritual vision versus spiritual blindness. This motif first shows up in Genesis 3, as Adam and Eve took of the forbidden fruit "and the eyes of both were opened" to experience what sin, guilt, and shame really are (Gen. 3:7), and the motif runs right through the Bible to the end of Revelation, where the New Jerusalem requires no created light by which to see, "for the glory of God gives it light, and its lamp is the Lamb" (Rev. 21:23). The prophet Isaiah gives prominent attention to this theme, and is quoted here in John 12 by Jesus (see also Matt. 13:14–15). Paul too quotes this same text from Isaiah in Acts 28:25–27 to explain rejection of God and his grace as blindness. John employs this theme of seeing versus blindness repeatedly throughout his Gospel as well as in his letters (e.g., John 3:3, 36; 6:30; 8:56; 9:1–41; 10:21; 11:37; 12:40; 14:19; 16:16–19; 1 John 2:11; 3:2). Jesus is "the light of the world" (John 8:12; 12:46). Only Jesus can cure the blindness of the human heart.

Theological Soundings

UNBELIEF. The ultimate human sin is unbelief. Unbelief is what drives all other sin. Adam and Eve sinned in the garden of Eden because of their unbelief, as they chose to not believe God's word and voice and instead believed the voice of the serpent (Satan). Here in John 12 we see highlighted this sin that shows up on nearly every page of the Bible and in every human heart: "Though he [Jesus] had done so many signs before them, they still did not believe in him" (John 12:37).

RESCUE. Speaking of his death by crucifixion, Jesus says in John 12:32, "And I, when I am lifted up from the earth, will draw all people to myself." Here Jesus gets at the heart of the whole Bible. Jesus views people as captives to sin, people in need of a rescue. Jesus and the Scriptures repeatedly underscore that sinners are unable to save themselves. We are helpless unless someone helps us from the outside. Jesus came to rescue us, and he did it in the most shocking manner—he was lifted up on a cross so that we could be lifted up to God.

Personal Implications

Take time to reflect on the implications of John 12:20–50 for your own life today. Make notes below on the personal implications for your walk with the Lord of (1) the *Gospel Glimpses*, (2) the *Whole-Bible Connections*, (3) the *Theological Soundings*, and (4) this passage as a whole.

1. Gospel Glimpses

2. Whole-Bible Connections

3. Theological Soundings

4. John 12:20–50

As You Finish This Unit . . .

Take a moment now to ask for the Lord's blessing and help as you engage in this study of John. And take a moment also to look back through this unit of study, to reflect on a few key things that the Lord may be teaching you—and perhaps to highlight or underline these to review again in the future.

Definitions

[1] **Substitutionary atonement** – The core reason for Jesus' death on the cross: Jesus offered himself to die as a substitute for believers. He took upon himself the punishment they deserve and thereby reconciled them to God.

[2] **Son of Man** – The title Jesus uses more than any other to refer to himself (e.g., Matt. 8:20; 11:19). While labeling himself this way may underscore Jesus' humanity, the phrase is most significant in relation to the figure in Daniel 7 who receives supreme authority and an everlasting kingdom from God (compare Dan. 7:13–14 and Matt. 26:64; Mark 14:62).

[3] **Satan** – A spiritual being whose name means "accuser." As the leader of all the demonic forces, he opposes God's rule and seeks to harm God's people and accuse them of wrongdoing. His power, however, is confined to the bounds that God has set for him, and one day he will be destroyed along with all his demons (Matt. 25:41; Rev. 20:10).

Week 8:
Jesus' Final Teaching
and Prayer

John 13:1–17:26

The Place of the Passage

Chapter 13 marks a transition into the second half of John's Gospel. John 13–21 zeroes in on Jesus' final few days leading to his death and resurrection. Having been rejected by the Jews, Jesus turns his attention to his new messianic community (his disciples). He prepares his disciples for the time to come after his resurrection and ascension to the Father. Jesus cleanses his disciples, teaches his disciples, and prays for his disciples. This "Farewell Discourse" (John 13–17) is unique to John's Gospel.

The Big Picture

In John 13:1–17:26 Jesus cleanses, teaches, and prays for his disciples, preparing them for the time when he is gone, exalted to be with the Father.

Reflection and Discussion

Read through the complete passage for this study, John 13:1–17:26. Then review the questions below and write your notes on them concerning this phase of Jesus' ministry. (For further background, see the *ESV Study Bible*, pages 2050–2060; also available online at www.esvbible.org.)

Jesus washes his disciples' feet to demonstrate his love for them, to set an example of servanthood, and to symbolize the washing away of sins through his death. Startlingly, Jesus washes all of his disciples' feet, including the feet of the one about to betray him—Judas. This scene is also unexpected because in first-century Jewish culture, footwashing was a task reserved for non-Jewish slaves. Here we have the Savior of the world washing the dirty feet of ordinary men, including the man about to betray him. What does this scene teach us about Jesus? What sticks out to you the most about this scene?

Humble · Servant
Jesus knows what's going to happen
but is so loving & caring

Note the events and words surrounding Judas's departure from the disciples in order to betray Jesus (13:21–30). How does Jesus feel, what does Jesus say, and what does Jesus know? What happens to Judas before leaving, and how does John 13:2 relate to 13:27? How do the other disciples react to what's going on? What do you make of John's closing words, "And it was night"?

He is troubled in Spirit
He knows what lies ahead & how he
will be betrayed.

The devil worked through Judas

According to John 13:34, how does Jesus want his disciples to love one another? According to John 13:35, what is the result of such love? In light of Jesus' subsequent death, what does it mean to love one another "just as" Jesus has loved?

"as I have loved you"

All men will know you are His disciples

even to death

Jesus says something startling to his disciples: "Truly, truly, I say to you, whoever believes in me will also do the works that I do; and greater works than these will he do, because I am going to the Father" (John 14:12). Because of the work Jesus is about to accomplish on the cross, and because God would send his Spirit to the church after Jesus' ascension,[1] Jesus tells his disciples that they will, in a sense, exercise a greater ministry than his. What do you think Jesus means by this statement? From what you know about the book of Acts, what takes place in Acts and in the early church that did not take place in Jesus' ministry?

They will spread the Word

Church grew - the Word spread

According to John 14:15, what would Jesus' disciples do if they loved him? According to 14:24, what is the identifying mark of those who do not love Jesus?

Keep His commandments

They will be obey His teachings

Love

61

Review Jesus' words about the Holy Spirit in John 14:15–26 and 16:4–15. According to these verses, who is the Holy Spirit, and what does he do?

The present tense of God.
Makes God real to us.
Advocate F

In John 15 Jesus gives the last of his seven "I am . . . " sayings. Summarize in a sentence what Jesus teaches in the metaphor that is used throughout this chapter.

Jesus is the vine   we are branches
connected to the vine we bear fruit.

According to John 15:8, how do people glorify God and prove their allegiance to Jesus?

Bear fruit Serving

Gal. 5:22

Jesus shares a wonderful reason for why he gives this Farewell Discourse to his disciples (John 15:11). How does this reason expand your conception of Jesus and what it means to follow him?

Joy may be in you – complete

Jesus – offers – Joy

John 17 narrates Jesus' final prayer. Speaking to his Father, who had sent him to earth, Jesus gives an account of his earthly mission. Jesus prays for himself, then for his disciples, and finally for later believers. Write down five truths this prayer teaches us.

Himself, Disciples & believers

1. Give eternal life

Glorify God by keeping us from sin.

God & Jesus One

Read through the following three sections on *Gospel Glimpses*, *Whole-Bible Connections*, and *Theological Soundings*. Then take time to reflect on the *Personal Implications* this passage from John may have for your walk with the Lord.

▶ Gospel Glimpses

THE WAY. One of the disciples, Thomas, asked Jesus how to get to heaven, into the presence of God. Jesus replied, "I am the way, and the truth, and the life. No one comes to the Father except through me" (John 14:6). This is good news! While on the one hand this statement from Jesus is hard news—there is one exclusive way to know God, and it is only through Jesus—it is also liberating news. Jesus is declaring the gospel here, the news that sinners can have a relationship with God and a place in heaven not through hard-wrought effort, but through casting themselves on the merit of Jesus. The way to heaven, Jesus says, is through himself. The way to heaven isn't to work harder and do more, but rather to trust that Jesus has done the work for us. He made a way for us. Jesus is the mediator[2] between God and sinful humanity.

JOY. In John 15:11, Jesus explains why he instructs his followers: "These things I have spoken to you, that my joy may be in you, and that your joy may be full." Joy! The reason Jesus came to earth and the reason Jesus instructs and leads us is for our joy, so that our joy "may be full." In Jesus we have a master, a Lord, who sets us free. This is unique to Christianity. Only Christianity tells of a God who calls his followers to know and obey him for the sake of their own joy. Jesus went to a cross so that you and I, sinners though we are, may be restored to God—and to real joy.

Whole-Bible Connections

LOVE. In John 13:34–35 Jesus calls his disciples to love one another, announcing that this is a "new commandment." At one level, these words of Jesus are not new; they are rooted in the Mosaic commands to love the Lord with all one's might and to love one's neighbor as oneself (Lev. 19:18; Deut. 6:5). But here Jesus deepens and expands this commandment. What is new about this commandment is that Jesus calls his disciples to love one another "just as I have loved you." This takes the call to love into a whole new realm. Jesus now calls his followers to a sacrificial love—a love he supremely demonstrated on the cross.

FRUITFUL. When God created Adam and Eve in the Garden of Eden, he instructed them to be fruitful (Gen. 1:28). Later God gave Israel the same commandment; the nation was called to be a fruitful tree, but they failed: "When I would gather them, declares the Lord, there are no grapes on the vine, nor figs on the fig tree; even the leaves are withered" (Jer. 8:13; see also Hos. 9:10, 16; Joel 1:7). In John 15, Jesus teaches the secret of fruitfulness: to abide in him. We are branches that can bear fruit as long as we are connected to the vine, Jesus. Jesus, however, went to the cross—was judged and treated as "fruitless"—so that fallen and unfruitful people like us can become the fruitful branches we were meant to be.

Theological Soundings

HOLY SPIRIT. In this section of John, Jesus talks repeatedly about the Holy Spirit. As Jesus instructs his disciples on how to live and minister subsequent to his ascension, he emphasizes the point that only through the power of the Holy Spirit can his disciples carry out their mission to the world. Jesus refers to the Holy Spirit as a "Helper" (John 14:16) who will dwell in, guide, and empower his disciples. The entire New Testament emphasizes what Jesus emphasizes here: the Christian life cannot be lived apart from the indwelling of the Holy Spirit, the third person of the Trinity.

HEAVEN. In John 14 Jesus speaks of heaven as "my Father's house" (14:2). Jesus tells his disciples that he is going to heaven in order to prepare a place for them, in order to eventually bring them there. Scripture[3] regularly talks about heaven. It's the place where believers live in God's presence after death. The words Jesus uses to describe heaven here in John are significant, as they express the personal manner in which Jesus cares for his disciples in order to bring them safely home to heaven.

Personal Implications

Take time to reflect on the implications of John 13:1–17:26 for your own life today. Make notes below on the personal implications for your walk with the Lord of (1) the *Gospel Glimpses*, (2) the *Whole-Bible Connections*, (3) the *Theological Soundings*, and (4) this passage as a whole.

1. Gospel Glimpses

2. Whole-Bible Connections

3. Theological Soundings

4. John 13:1–17:26

As You Finish This Unit . . .

Take a moment now to ask for the Lord's blessing and help as you engage in this study of John. And take a moment also to look back through this unit of study, to reflect on a few key things that the Lord may be teaching you—and perhaps to highlight or underline these to review again in the future.

Definitions

[1] **Ascension** – The departure of the resurrected, glorified Jesus to God the Father in heaven (Luke 24:50–51; Acts 1:6–11).

[2] **Mediator** – One who intercedes between parties to resolve a conflict or achieve a goal. Jesus is the mediator between God and rebellious humanity (1 Tim. 2:5; compare Heb. 9:15; 12:24).

[3] **Scripture** – Writings regarded by Christians as inspired by God and authoritative in all areas of doctrine and practice.

WEEK 9:
JESUS' ARREST, TRIAL, DEATH, AND BURIAL

John 18:1–19:42

▲

John's Gospel now hurtles toward Jesus' crucifixion.[1] After being betrayed by Judas, Jesus receives an informal hearing before the Jewish leadership and a Roman trial before Pilate. He is then crucified and buried. All of John has been leading toward this climactic section of his Gospel.

The Big Picture

In John 18:1–19:42 the Son of God is betrayed, crucified, and buried.

Reflection and Discussion

Read through the complete passage for this study, John 18:1–19:42. Then review the three sections below and write your notes on the questions concerning this climactic phase of Jesus' ministry. (For further background, see the *ESV Study Bible*, pages 2060–2068; also available online at www.esvbible.org.)

1. Jesus Is Betrayed (18:1–11)

Judas, the betrayer, approaches Jesus with soldiers, lanterns, torches, and weapons. Jesus boldly walks forward and approaches his captors. Once they state that they are looking for "Jesus of Nazareth," Jesus replies, "I am he," and immediately his captors draw back and fall to the ground. Falling to the ground is a common reaction to divine revelation. Jesus' captors fall to the ground because his self-identification, "I am he," has connotations of deity (see, for example, John 6:20; 8:24; 8:58). Review also Ezekiel 1:28, Acts 9:4, and Revelation 1:17. How do these passages illuminate this scene?

Voice from heaven - likeness of glory of the Lord
Acts 9:4 - Saul's conversion, Jesus appears to Saul light

Rebuking Peter for his use of the sword, Jesus says, "Put your sword into its sheath; shall I not drink the cup that the Father has given me?" (John 18:11). Explain the meaning of Jesus' words. What is the cup the Father has given him? To color in your answer, reference Psalm 75:8, Isaiah 51:17, and Jeremiah 25:15–17.

Judgment - cup of wrath
God gives to all

2. Jesus Is Arrested and Tried (18:12–19:16)

Contrast John 13:37 with 18:15–18. What caused this disciple to change his stance?

Petros's denial.
Fearful of his life?

Pilate asks Jesus if he is "the King of the Jews" (John 18:33). Jesus answers Pilate, explaining the different nature of the kingdom of God.[2] What do we learn about this kingdom and this King from Jesus' words?

Truth

According to Jesus, where does Pilate's authority come from? Does Pilate think Jesus is guilty or innocent? Why does Pilate go forward with crucifying Jesus?

God
No
Fear of people

3. Jesus Is Crucified (19:16–42)

John makes frequent use of double meaning and irony in his Gospel. Note two instances of irony in this section of John. First, it was once Pilate "sat down on the judgment seat" (19:13) that Pilate sentenced the Son of God to his crucifixion. Second, "Pilate also wrote an inscription and put it on the cross. It read, 'Jesus of Nazareth, the King of the Jews'" (19:19). This inscription was written in three languages, allowing the majority of people in the vicinity of Jerusalem to read it. What double meaning or irony do you see in these two events?

vs 16 - 15

Read Psalm 22, a psalm that prophesies the suffering of the Messiah. What key connections and fulfillments do you see between Psalm 22 and John's account of Jesus' crucifixion?

vs - 14 -18

What do we learn about Jesus from how he cares for his mother from the cross (19:25–27)? Why does Jesus do this?

Tender - Caring - Out of love

"It is finished" are the last words Jesus speaks from the cross (19:30). With these words Jesus announces the completion of the preeminent work the Father sent him to do; namely, his work of bearing the penalty for his people's sins. These three words are among the most powerful words in the Bible. Ponder and reflect on the finished work of Christ on the cross and how this finished work intersects with your own life today.

Read through the following three sections on *Gospel Glimpses, Whole-Bible Connections*, and *Theological Soundings*. Then take time to reflect on the *Personal Implications* this passage from John may have for your walk with the Lord.

▶ Gospel Glimpses

THE FATHER'S CUP. Instead of retaliating against his captors, Jesus said, "Shall I not drink the cup that the Father has given me?" (John 18:11). Jesus is referring to the cup of God's wrath against sinners. Psalm 75:8 states, "For in the hand of the LORD there is a cup with foaming wine, well mixed, and he pours out from it, and all the wicked of the earth shall drain it down to the dregs." This cup was meant for us. We, the sinful ones, deserve to drink this cup of wrath. But Jesus drank this cup in our place. At the cross the Father's wrath against sin was poured out on Jesus so that it need never be poured out on those who trust in him.

IMPERFECT DISCIPLES. John's Gospel highlights Jesus' imperfect disciples. Peter, the disciple who boldly proclaimed that he would lay down his life for Jesus (John 13:37), shamefully denies even being associated with Jesus once discipleship becomes costly (John 18). This is good news for us. After his resurrection Jesus forgives Peter and articulates his love for him (21:15–19). Jesus' original band of disciples were imperfect—so imperfect that the leader of Jesus' disciples went so far as to deny even knowing him. We, too, are imperfect disciples. And the same grace Jesus extended to Peter he extends to us.

SUBSTITUTION. Jesus' relationship with Barabbas illustrates the gospel. Instead of punishing Barabbas, "a robber" (John 18:40) and thus guilty of a serious crime, Jesus is substituted for Barabbas. Instead of Barabbas going to the cross, Jesus went to the cross. Jesus was punished and Barabbas was set free. This is the gospel story. We are guilty of serious crime against God, and we deserve punishment by death. But Jesus has taken the punishment for us. He substituted himself for us so that we could live.

▶ Whole-Bible Connections

THE LAMB OF GOD. John's Gospel begins with John the Baptist's introduction to Jesus: "Behold, the Lamb of God, who takes away the sin of the world!" (John 1:29). Jesus' crucifixion occurred on "the day of Preparation of the Passover" (John 19:14), the day when Passover lambs would be sacrificed in Jerusalem.

The Passover celebration stretches back many centuries before the coming of Christ. God's people, Israel, were captives in Egypt. The Passover meal was the meal God's people ate on the night they were set free from Egyptian captivity (Exodus 12). The blood of the Passover lamb protected Israel from God's wrath, for homes that had the blood of the Passover lamb smeared on their doorposts and lintel were "passed over" and spared of God's judgment. Crucified at Passover, Jesus' blood is smeared on a cross, allowing God's wrath to pass over all who trust in the Lamb of God.

PROPHECY FULFILLED. In chapter 19 John quotes Psalm 22 (the psalm most frequently quoted in the New Testament), in which the psalmist writes many prophetic details of the execution scene that are fulfilled here in Jesus' death, nearly a thousand years later. When the Roman soldiers divided Jesus' garments and cast lots for his tunic, they unknowingly fulfilled Scripture. This is a theme John regularly highlights—the unwitting participation of Jesus' enemies in God's plan of redemption.[3] Jesus' crucifixion as told by John contains several striking connections with Psalm 22, including the casting of lots for the sufferer's clothing (v. 18), the sufferer's thirst (v. 15), and the "pierced ... hands and feet" (v. 16).

Theological Soundings

THE KINGDOM OF GOD. At his trial Jesus speaks about the kingdom of God. Scripture teaches that no matter what appears to be happening among the various kingdoms of this world, God is the true king of this world, the king of both heaven and earth. God's kingdom is sovereign[4] over every earthly kingdom. In his providential and mysterious way, God exercises his rule even through the most wicked earthly kingdoms. Jesus' crucifixion perfectly illustrates this point. Pilate says to Jesus, "Do you not know that I have authority to release you and authority to crucify you?" (John 19:10). Yet Jesus replied to Pilate, "You would have no authority over me at all unless it had been given you from above" (John 19:11). While Pilate and the Roman government call for the crucifixion of the Son of God, it is God who first granted this authority to this earthly kingdom. God is always in charge.

Personal Implications

Take time to reflect on the implications of John 18:1–19:42 for your own life today. Make notes below on the personal implications for your walk with the Lord of (1) the *Gospel Glimpses*, (2) the *Whole-Bible Connections*, (3) the *Theological Soundings*, and (4) this passage as a whole.

1. Gospel Glimpses

2. Whole-Bible Connections

3. Theological Soundings

4. John 18:1–19:42

As You Finish This Unit . . .

Take a moment now to ask for the Lord's blessing and help as you engage in this study of John. And take a moment also to look back through this unit of study, to reflect on a few key things that the Lord may be teaching you—and perhaps to highlight or underline these to review again in the future.

Definitions

[1] **Crucifixion** – A means of execution in which the person was fastened, by ropes or nails, to a crossbeam that was then raised and attached to a vertical beam, forming a cross (the root meaning of "crucifixion"). The process was designed to maximize pain and humiliation, and to serve as a deterrent for other potential offenders. Jesus suffered this form of execution (Matt. 27:32–56), not for any offense he had committed (Heb. 4:15) but as the atoning sacrifice for all who would believe in him (John 3:16).

[2] **Kingdom of God** – The sovereign rule of God. At the present time, the fallen, sinful world does not belong to the kingdom of God, since it does not submit to God's rule. Instead, God's kingdom can be found in heaven and among his people (Matt. 6:9–10; Luke 17:20–21). After Christ returns, however, the kingdom of the world will become the kingdom of God (Rev. 11:15). Then all people will, either willingly or regretfully, acknowledge his sovereignty (Phil. 2:9–11). Even the natural world will be transformed to operate in perfect harmony with God (Rom. 8:19–23).

[3] **Redemption** – In the context of the Bible, the act of buying back someone who had become enslaved or something that had been lost to someone else. Through his death and resurrection, Jesus purchased redemption for all believers (Col. 1:13–14).

[4] **Sovereignty** – Supreme and independent power and authority. Sovereignty over all things is a distinctive attribute of God (1 Tim. 6:15–16). He directs all things to carry out his purposes (Rom. 8:28–29).

74

WEEK 10:
JESUS' RESURRECTION
AND APPEARANCES

John 20:1–29

▲

John 19 ends with the Son of God crucified, dead, and buried in a tomb. John 20 begins with the Son of God alive, having been raised from death itself. The tone of John's Gospel dramatically shifts in John 20. This is the hinge on which the entire Gospel account pivots. Jesus is alive, and he now appears to his disciples and commissions them for ministry.

The Big Picture

John 20:1–29 recounts Jesus' resurrection from the dead, his encounter with Mary Magdalene and the disciples, and his commissioning of the disciples.

> **Reflection and Discussion**

Read through the complete passage for this study, John 20:1–29. Then review the questions below and write your notes on them concerning this phase of Jesus' ministry. (For further background, see the *ESV Study Bible*, pages 2068–2071; also available online at www.esvbible.org.)

Jesus' resurrection takes place "on the first day of the week" (20:1). Thus the early Christians set aside Sunday as the day for gathering and worship (Acts 20:7; 1 Cor. 16:2). What does this say about how Christians are to view their work week? Do we rest from work, living for the weekend, or do we "work from rest," gaining strength for our work from our times of worship?

Mary Magdalene is the first to visit Jesus' tomb. Upon finding that the stone had been rolled away from the tomb, Mary "ran" to tell the news to Peter and the disciple "whom Jesus loved" (John, the author of this Gospel). What does Mary communicate to these two disciples; how does she explain the empty tomb? What do Peter and John do once they hear the news from Mary?

They have taken away my Lord

Verse 8 signals a change. What happens to John once he enters the tomb? Why do you think the disciples, Peter and John, went back to their homes (v. 10)? With whom might John have shared the good news? Recall John 19:27.

Mary stays at the tomb and weeps. Two angels[1] appear and ask Mary a question. Mary answers the question. Then, Jesus appears and asks Mary the same question the angels asked. Who does Mary think Jesus is? What does it take for Mary to recognize Jesus? From what you know of first-century Jewish culture, why might it be significant that a woman is the first one to encounter the resurrected Jesus?

Gardiner

Jesus knows my name

Later that same day, at nighttime, Jesus appears to his disciples. Why do his disciples have the doors locked? What does Jesus say to his disciples, what does he show his disciples, and how do his disciples respond?

Fearful

After showing his disciples his hands and his side, Jesus commissions his disciples. The sent one (Jesus) has now become the sender, commissioning his disciples to serve as his messengers and empowering them with the Holy Spirit. How do you see all three members of the Trinity involved in this scene? How does this notion of being "sent" by Jesus help deepen your understanding of Christian discipleship?

John 20:21–22 is John's version of the Great Commission. Compare this passage with Matthew's (Matt. 28:16–20) version of the Great Commission. What similarities and what differences do you notice?

Sending - Go   Posting mandate

Commissions   Teaching

Not alone

Eight days after Jesus' first encounter with the disciples, how does Jesus handle Thomas's doubt? How does Thomas respond to his encounter with Jesus? Through this encounter, what does Jesus teach his disciples about faith?[2]

Read through the following three sections on *Gospel Glimpses, Whole-Bible Connections,* and *Theological Soundings.* Then take time to reflect on the *Personal Implications* this passage from John may have for your walk with the Lord.

Gospel Glimpses

THE DEATH OF DEATH. Jesus defeated death. The world and Satan gave Jesus their best shot—betrayal, beatings, crucifixion, death, and burial. But it couldn't hold Jesus. Even death couldn't defeat him. Jesus died; he took a final breath; he was wrapped in burial clothes and placed in a tomb. And on a Sunday morning, Jesus stood outside his tomb, resurrected and alive. This is our Savior—the Son of God who defeated death. Do you think God and his gospel are not powerful enough to rescue you from what enslaves and shames you? Meditate on the empty tomb. God raised Jesus from the dead; he can certainly raise you out of your tomb.

MY FATHER AND YOUR FATHER. Encountering Mary after his resurrection, Jesus gave Mary instructions: "Go to my brothers and say to them, 'I am ascending to my Father and your Father, to my God and your God'" (John 20:17). This is good news! Because of Jesus' life, death, resurrection, and ascension, Jesus' disciples can now call God "Father." Throughout the Old Testament God's people did not speak of God as "Father," for the Messiah had not yet come to make a full atonement[3] for sins. But with the finished work of Jesus, we can now know God in the most intimate sense, as our Father. The finished work of Jesus turns sinners into sons and daughters of the almighty God.

HOPE FOR THE DOUBTING. Thomas, one of Jesus' disciples, doubted whether or not Jesus really rose from the dead. Instead of condemning Thomas, the risen Jesus came to Thomas and gave him proof that silenced all doubts. The dominant note in this scene is that of a grace-filled, humble Savior who knows our doubts and takes action to help us overcome them.

Whole-Bible Connections

THE SERPENT CRUSHER. After Adam and Eve's sin in the garden of Eden, God promised that Adam and Eve's line would continue and that one day, a descendant of Adam and Eve would crush the serpent, Satan (Gen. 3:15). The whole Bible is, from one standpoint, the story of the search for the serpent crusher, the coming king who would conquer God's enemies and defeat Satan and death. John's Gospel highlights Jesus as the offspring who has finally conquered Satan. Sin, Satan, and death were decisively defeated when Jesus rose from the dead.

THE SPIRIT POURED OUT. Long before the arrival of Jesus, Joel prophesied that one day God would pour out his Spirit on his people. "And it shall come to pass afterward, that I will pour out my Spirit on all flesh; your sons and your daughters shall prophesy, your old men shall dream dreams, and your young men shall see visions. Even on the male and female servants in those days I will pour out my Spirit" (Joel 2:28–29). Here in John we see that this day begins to dawn. One of the first things Jesus does after his resurrection is go to his disciples and breathe on them, giving them the Holy Spirit (John 20:22). This is a foretaste of what will happen later in Acts 2, when the Holy Spirit falls upon God's people in even greater measure, enabling and empowering them to be a light to a dark world.

Theological Soundings

RESURRECTION. The Scriptures teach that everyone who dies will be resurrected. The wicked—those who refused to trust in God—will be resurrected to judgment.[4] And the righteous[5]—those who trusted in God—will be resurrected to eternal life (John 5:29). Those raised will be given new, physical bodies. For the redeemed, resurrection life will be a return to Eden, with no more sickness, sadness, or death—and without even the possibility of sin.

THE MISSIONARY TRINITY. All three members of the Trinity are involved in Jesus' commissioning of his disciples—the Father, the Son, and the Holy Spirit (John 20:21–23). With the full involvement of the Trinity, Jesus' disciples are commissioned to be his messengers on earth, to spread the gospel of the forgiveness of sins through Jesus (v. 23). More than the other Gospel writers, John highlights the missionary nature of God's work in the gospel. All three persons of the Trinity are concerned to reach people with the good news of God's great love.

Personal Implications

Take time to reflect on the implications of John 20:1–29 for your own life today. Make notes below on the personal implications for your walk with the Lord of (1) the *Gospel Glimpses*, (2) the *Whole-Bible Connections*, (3) the *Theological Soundings*, and (4) this passage as a whole.

1. Gospel Glimpses

2. Whole-Bible Connections

3. Theological Soundings

4. John 20:1–29

As You Finish This Unit . . .

Take a moment now to ask for the Lord's blessing and help as you engage in this study of John. And take a moment also to look back through this unit of study, to reflect on a few key things that the Lord may be teaching you—and perhaps to highlight or underline these to review again in the future.

Definitions

[1] **Angel** – A supernatural messenger of God, often sent to carry out his will or to assist human beings in carrying out his will. Though angels are more powerful than humans and often instill awe, they are not to be worshiped (Col. 2:18; Rev. 22:8–9). The Bible does, however, note certain appearances of an "angel of the Lord" which are apparently a physical manifestation of God himself.

[2] **Faith** – Trust in or reliance upon something or someone despite a lack of concrete proof. Salvation, which is purely a work of God's grace, can be received only through faith (Rom. 5:2; Eph. 2:8–9). The writer of Hebrews calls on believers to emulate those who lived godly lives by faith (Hebrews 11).

[3] **Atonement** – The reconciliation of a person with God, often associated with the offering of a sacrifice. Through his death and resurrection, Jesus Christ made atonement for the sins of believers. His death satisfied God's just wrath against sinful humanity, just as OT sacrifices symbolized substitutionary death as payment for sin.

[4] **Judgment** – Any assessment of something or someone, especially moral assessment. The Bible also speaks of a final day of judgment when Christ returns, when all those who have refused to repent will be judged (Rev. 20:12–15).

[5] **Righteous** – The quality of being morally right and without sin. One of God's distinctive attributes. God imputes righteousness to (justifies) those who trust in Jesus Christ.

Week 11:
Purpose Statement
and Epilogue

John 20:30–21:25

▲

The Place of the Passage

This passage brings John's Gospel to a close. The Gospel concludes with a purpose statement and epilogue which together rehearse the major themes of the Gospel: Jesus' identity as the Christ and Son of God, his messianic signs, the urgency of believing in Jesus, and the gift of eternal life. John's Gospel closes with Jesus' third and final resurrection appearance recorded by John, an encounter that highlights the respective callings of Peter and John, "the disciple whom Jesus loved."

The Big Picture

John 20:30–21:25 recounts the major themes of John's Gospel and narrates Jesus' resurrection appearance to his disciples.

Reflection and Discussion

Read through the complete passage for this study, John 20:30–21:25. Then review the questions below and write your notes on them concerning this phase of Jesus' ministry. (For further background, see the *ESV Study Bible*, pages 2071–2072; also available online at www.esvbible.org.)

John 20:30–31 states the purpose for which John wrote this Gospel. What major themes are touched upon in this purpose statement?

"that you may believe ... because you have seen ..."

How should this purpose statement inform how Christians read, study, preach, and interact with this book?

John 21 narrates the third resurrection appearance by Jesus recorded by John. Which disciples are present for this encounter? How do the disciples recognize Jesus?

Peter, Thomas, Nathanael, sons of Zebedee & 2 others

When He told them to cast their nets on the other side of the boat & more and overwhelmed

What do you make of the fact that Jesus' final resurrection appearance with his disciples is a breakfast meeting? What similarities do you see between this scene, Jesus' first sign (John 2), and the famous sign recorded in John 6:1–15?

2:1 - Turning water into wine

6 - Bread of life.

Jesus appears in the ordinary experiences of life.

Think about the three resurrection appearances Jesus has made to his disciples (John 20:19–23; 24–29; 21:1–14). What have each of these three appearances uniquely communicated?

Peter denied Jesus three times (John 18:15–18, 25–27). Here Jesus asks Peter three times if he loves him (21:15-17). What is Jesus doing?

Instructing Peter to "feed my sheep," Jesus gives Peter his calling to shepherd the church.[1] How do you see grace in this dialogue between Jesus and Peter and in the responsibility Jesus gives to Peter?

After being handed his calling from Jesus, Peter asks Jesus about the calling on John's life. What does this scene teach us about the unique callings God gives his people? What lessons are Jesus' words of response to Peter's question meant to teach him, and us through him?

John beautifully ends his Gospel with statements that stir the imagination. How does John 21:25 affect your imagination? What is this verse communicating about the ministry of Jesus?

Endless beyond description

Each of the Gospel writers communicates something unique to their audience with the ending of their Gospel. How does John's ending affect you, and how is this different from the endings of the other Gospel accounts?

Read through the following three sections on *Gospel Glimpses*, *Whole-Bible Connections*, and *Theological Soundings*. Then take time to reflect on the *Personal Implications* this passage from John may have for your walk with the Lord.

Gospel Glimpses

LORD OF THE ORDINARY. Jesus does many ordinary things. Jesus' first miracle recorded in the Gospel of John is turning water into wine—keeping a festive wedding party going. And Jesus' final scene in John shows him cooking breakfast for his disciples. Fully God and fully man, Jesus knows the human condition. He knows our ordinary lives, our ordinary fears, and our busy schedules. Through it all, he injects joy, caring even for our physical needs.

GRACE. Peter boldly declared to Jesus that he was ready to lay down his life for him (John 13:37). Yet once he was required to put his own safety at risk, Peter denied knowing Jesus. He did this three times. After Jesus' resurrection from the dead, however, Jesus talks to Peter about love three times. In this way he is reinstating Peter as his disciple. And Jesus does more than that. He gives Peter an enormous responsibility, commanding him to shepherd and lead the church. This is extraordinary—the man who had recently denied Jesus at the hour when Jesus needed him most has now been forgiven by Jesus and entrusted with the responsibility to lead others toward Jesus. This is grace. This is how God's economy works.

LOVED. Throughout his Gospel, John has identified himself as "the disciple whom Jesus loved." Why do you suppose he does that? This, however, is not a title reserved for John. This is a title true of all who trust in Jesus for the forgiveness of sins. Every disciple of Jesus can call themselves "the disciple whom Jesus loved."

Whole-Bible Connections

GOD'S GREATNESS. Nearly every page of the Bible testifies to the grandness of God and God's work. The Bible begins with astonishing news: God created the universe simply through the power of his word. The Bible ends with astonishing news: Jesus will return to earth at the roar of the trumpet and will bring heaven down to earth, forever changing life as we know it. And John ends his Gospel with similar astonishment, with a statement that makes the reader see just how big Jesus really is. In twenty-one chapters John has chronicled a great deal of Jesus' teaching and action, yet John states, "Now there are also many other things that Jesus did. Were every one of them to be written, I suppose that the world itself could not contain the books that would be written" (21:25). John's aim is for his readers to behold how glorious Jesus is. The mighty works of God come to a climax here in John 21:25; it is not possible to record fully the magnitude and extent of who Jesus is and what he has accomplished.

A GREAT FEAST. "Come and have breakfast," said Jesus to his worn-out disciples (John 21:12). At the beginning of the Bible, God's people (Adam and Eve) are free to eat from all the trees of Eden except one. At the end of the Bible, God's people (the church) are once more invited to eat from the flourishing tree of life (Rev. 22:2). And all through the Bible, from Genesis to Revelation, the great joy that God has for his people is depicted in terms of a feast (e.g., Isa. 25:6; 30:29; Jer. 31:14; Luke 14:12–24). While on one level the new earth will no doubt include the enjoyment of physical foods, this enjoyment itself serves as a glimpse of the greatest joy of all: knowing God through Jesus, the Bread of Life (John 6:35).

Theological Soundings

ALL-KNOWING. As Jesus peppers him with questions, Peter states, "Lord, you know everything" (John 21:17). Peter is right. After witnessing the resurrection, Peter now knows that Jesus is Lord and that he knows everything. God (Father, Son, and Holy Spirit) is omniscient.[2] He knows everything at all times. God is not limited in his knowledge. Nothing escapes his knowledge and providence.[3] Elsewhere Jesus states that not even a sparrow can fall to the ground apart from God's knowledge and will (Matt. 10:29).

VOCATION. Laced throughout the Bible is the doctrine of vocation, the truth that God creates everyone uniquely (Psalm 139) and places unique callings on each individual life. We see this in the final chapter of John's Gospel. Jesus states that Peter and John have different yet equally strategic ways that their lives are to be used for the glory of God. The doctrine of vocation is all about how God does his work in the world—namely, through his unique human creations. We should not feel pressure to compare ourselves to others, for God has given a unique calling to each one of us that only we can uniquely fulfill. Peter was called to be Peter. John was called to be John. You are called to be you.

Personal Implications

Take time to reflect on the implications of John 20:30–21:25 for your own life today. Make notes below on the personal implications for your walk with the Lord of (1) the *Gospel Glimpses*, (2) the *Whole-Bible Connections*, (3) the *Theological Soundings*, and (4) this passage as a whole.

1. Gospel Glimpses

2. Whole-Bible Connections

3. Theological Soundings

4. John 20:30–21:25

> ## As You Finish This Unit . . .

Take a moment now to ask for the Lord's blessing and help as you engage in this study of John. And take a moment also to look back through this unit of study, to reflect on a few key things that the Lord may be teaching you—and perhaps to highlight or underline these to review again in the future.

Definitions

[1] **Church** – From a Greek word meaning "assembly." The church is the body of believers in Jesus Christ. The word can refer either to all believers everywhere or to a local gathering of believers.

[2] **Omniscient** – An attribute of God that describes his complete knowledge and understanding of all things at all times.

[3] **Providence** – God's good, wise, and sovereign guidance and control of all things, by which he supplies all our needs and accomplishes his holy will.

WEEK 12:
SUMMARY AND
CONCLUSION

▲

As we draw this study of John to a close, we begin by summing up the big picture of John's Gospel as a whole. We will then review some questions for reflection in light of John's entire account, with a final identification of Gospel Glimpses, Whole-Bible Connections, and Theological Soundings, all with a view to seeing the Gospel of John in its entirety.

The Big Picture of John

Over the course of this study we have seen that John's Gospel falls roughly into two sections.

The first section of John (1:1–12:50) spotlights Jesus' messianic identity by identifying the many "signs" he performed, climaxing with the raising of Lazarus from the dead. This section also features the teaching of Jesus, as Jesus reveals his identity as the messianic Son of God. Conflict with the Jewish leaders escalates. Along the way, John highlights that Jesus was "sent" by God to rescue a dark world.

The second section of John (13:1–21:25) narrates the intensifying conflict between Jesus and the Jewish leaders and also Jesus' Farewell Discourse. The book then culminates in Jesus' betrayal, crucifixion, burial, resurrection, and resurrection appearances. Jesus then sends his disciples to be light in a dark world.

Putting both sections together, the Gospel of John shows us that Jesus is "the Lamb of God who takes away the sin of the world" (John 1:29). John shows us that in Jesus, God has provided redemption for his people. Jesus came as the fulfillment of the Old Testament promises of a coming king and shepherd. He was not the king or shepherd they expected (a king of political triumph); he was the shepherd they most desperately needed—"I am the good shepherd. The good shepherd lays down his life for the sheep" (John 10:11). Through faith in Jesus and his work on our behalf, we are granted "new birth," reconciled to God, filled with the Holy Spirit, and brought into God's kingdom. John's Gospel speaks of our missionary God, who sent Jesus to us, and of our missionary calling as Jesus now sends us into the world.

Read through the following three sections on *Gospel Glimpses, Whole-Bible Connections*, and *Theological Soundings*. Then take time to reflect on the *Personal Implications* these sections may have for your walk with the Lord.

Gospel Glimpses

Throughout John's Gospel we have seen the grace of God in the gospel. Jesus has extended grace to sinners of all stripes. He has melted with compassion over the sight of human sin and suffering. He has challenged the emptiness of the arid religion of the scribes and Pharisees, earning their opposition as a result. Repeatedly Jesus has flipped inside out our natural understanding of how to relate to God. We don't have to build a ladder to heaven to know God, for in Jesus God has extended a ladder down to us. Living under the glad favor of God isn't a result of effort, hard work, or morality. It is the sheer miracle of grace—receiving new birth through the finished work of Jesus Christ. The message of John's Gospel is summed up in Jesus' bold words from the cross, "It is finished" (John 19:30).

Has your understanding of the gospel changed, expanded, or deepened in any particular way during the course of this study? Explain.

Be affirmation

What are a few particular passages in John that have brought the gospel home to you in a new way? Why have these texts helped you better grasp the gospel of God's grace?

1:14

Whole-Bible Connections

John presents Jesus as God in the flesh (1:14), the revealer of the Father (14:9), and the messianic King (1:41, 49; 4:25; 6:15), answering many Old Testament hopes. Repeatedly John shows how Jesus fulfills the prophecies, promises, and longings of the Old Testament, especially its promises of everlasting salvation. Jesus brings the entire Old Testament to decisive fulfillment, as John the Baptist declares at the very beginning of the Gospel: "Behold, the Lamb of God, who takes away the sin of the world!" (1:29).

How has your understanding of how John's Gospel fits within the entire Bible been deepened through your study of John?

What are some connections in John to the Old Testament that you hadn't noticed before?

In the beginning

Has your understanding of the unity of the Bible been clarified through studying John? How so?

What development has there been in your view of who Jesus is and how he fulfills the Old Testament?

Theological Soundings

John contributes much to Christian theology. Doctrines that are reinforced and clarified in John include the preexistence of Christ, the deity of Christ, human sin, the Trinity, the Holy Spirit, the atonement, resurrection, heaven and hell, divine sovereignty, the kingdom of God, and the missionary nature of God's people.

94

Where has your theology been tweaked, corrected, or enhanced as you have studied John?

How would our understanding of God be diminished if we did not have John's Gospel?

How does John's Gospel uniquely contribute to our understanding of Jesus?

What are a few specific ways in which John helps us understand the human condition?

Personal Implications

As you consider the Gospel of John as a whole, what implications do you see for your own life? Consider especially the issue of life in Christ. This is an important emphasis throughout John, particularly Jesus' emphasis that, just as the Father sent him into the world, so Jesus sends his disciples into the world as they abide in him. What are the ramifications for your own life of Jesus' teaching on discipleship in John?

Abide in Him. Sent

As you reflect on John as a whole, what other implications for your own life have arisen?

As You Finish Studying John . . .

We rejoice with you as you finish studying the book of John! May this study become part of your Christian walk of faith, day by day and week by week throughout all your life. Now we would greatly encourage you to continue to study the Word of God on a week-by-week basis. To continue your study of the Bible, we would encourage you to consider other books in the *Knowing the Bible* series, and to visit www.knowingthebibleseries.org.

Lastly, take a moment again to look back through this study of John, which you have undertaken during these recent weeks. Review again the notes that you have written, and the things that you have highlighted or underlined. Reflect again on the key themes that the Lord has been teaching you about himself and about his Word. May these things become a treasure for you throughout your life—which we pray will be true for you, in the name of the Father, and the Son, and the Holy Spirit. Amen.